Soul Vomit

Domestic Violence

Aftermath

ISBN-13: 978-0-9859028-6-5
ISBN-10: 0985902868

Published by Broken Publications
www.BrokenPublications.com

Edited by Jennifer-Crystal Johnson
www.JenniferCrystalJohnson.com

Cover art by Eleanor Leonne Bennett
www.EleanorLeonneBennett.com

Cover layout by Jennifer-Crystal Johnson
www.JenniferCrystalJohnson.com

For more about the Soul Vomit annual anthology, go to www.SoulVomit.com or follow us on Facebook at www.Facebook.com/SoulVomitAnthology.

A
Pacific Northwest
Publisher

Disclaimer:

This book is not intended as a substitute for the medical advice of physicians. The reader should regularly consult a physician in matters relating to his/her health and particularly with respect to any symptoms that may require diagnosis or medical attention.

This book is designed to provide information and motivation to our readers. Neither the publisher nor the authors shall be liable for any physical, psychological, emotional, financial, or commercial damages, including but not limited to special, incidental, consequential, or other damages. You are responsible for your own choices, actions, and results.

If you or someone you know is in a domestic violence situation, please get help!

Table of Contents

Foreword

Jennifer-Crystal Johnson

First and foremost, I want to say a big thank you to everyone who contributed to this anthology to make it a reality for the second time around. Without you, this book would not be possible.

I commend those of you who are reading this book, have purchased it in show of support, or are simply showing an interest in the often misunderstood and silent epidemic of domestic violence that happens behind closed doors all over the world every single day. It's not easy to read about... it's actually pretty uncomfortable in some cases. But if it were a comfortable topic, then it wouldn't be a problem, would it?

My mission in publishing this anthology is to bring to light some of the typical experiences of men and women suffering through abuse on a daily basis, as well as offer some clarification and insight about what people go through long after they leave an abuser. Soul Vomit was created to give a voice to victims who are still stuck, survivors who have gotten out and want to help make a difference by telling their story, and to serve as a warning to men and women everywhere that love isn't always sunshine and rainbows, nor is it always meant to last... nor is it enough on its own.

2014 has seen some pretty crazy stories in the news about domestic violence all over the world. Between scrutiny of the NFL for having so many domestic violence arrests and the wildly public case against Ray Rice, and the more recent announcement by South Carolina that the Stand Your Ground law doesn't apply to domestic violence victims, it's becoming more and more apparent that people in leadership positions aren't taking the issue as seriously as they should.

In other words, the very people who *should* be protecting and helping victims are making it easier for abusers to run rampant and get away with their despicable and hideous behavior. *This is not good.* I find it unacceptable and disgusting.

That's also why it renews my resolve to continue publishing this anthology and raising awareness as well as donation money for DV victims and survivors. The system is broken, and until people make enough noise to force repairs, those of us who can take a stand must become an even noisier and more annoying squeaky wheel.

It saddens me to think that we live in the information age, yet people still don't fully understand domestic violence or the incredible amount of pain and suffering it causes for victims, even for years and years after they are no longer with their abusers. I'm about nine years into my journey after leaving, and I have to tell you, I still have days when I struggle. Logically I know better, but emotionally, it's a very persistent monster, which is why I chose the theme of *Aftermath* for this year's anthology.

There are still pieces contained that portray abuse itself because it's important to remind people why there's aftermath in the first place. Domestic violence causes Post-Traumatic Stress Disorder, which has a lifelong effect on everyone it touches, be it through DV, wartime, an attack, an accident, or anything else life may throw at us. The biggest difference between domestic violence PTSD and other kinds?

It's caused by a person you love. A person who you think loves you.

People go into an actual warzone expecting battle and ready to shoot, usually with training under their belt. People go for a drive with their seatbelt on knowing there's a possibility of an accident, which is why people try to drive carefully and keep their distance from those who don't (I would hope so, anyway… there are always exceptions).

You go into a relationship or marriage expecting and hoping for your version of happily ever after with someone who you believe loves you… only to have a warzone slapped across your home life (where you're supposed to feel safe) with zero training, zero preparedness, and a dizzying confusion about what happened. It permeates everything. Every thought, worry, idea, and emotion begins to feel tainted because all you can think in the front of your mind is:

Will this thought piss him off? Wait… why would my thoughts piss him off? He can't read my mind… or can he? He seems to know when I'm thinking about leaving or do something wrong….

What will the consequences be for me if I decide to go to the store without him? Can I even do that? Am I even allowed? You know, I'd better not… I don't want to set him off.

I'd better hide the unfolded laundry so he doesn't start screaming at me….

If I have a white mocha instead of a regular will he think I went to coffee with someone else and tried it first?

Every single decision, thought, movement, word, emotion, outfit, book, song, website, meal, and so on becomes infected by this person. You end up feeling like you can't do anything right, so you do as you're told and not much else, hoping for as little backlash as possible. It's like being a prisoner inside your own body because, on the one hand, you love this person… on the other hand, you're terrified because he might just shoot you in the head like he said he would.

People think that if a victim leaves, that means it's all over. That is not the case, by any stretch of the imagination. In a way, it has just begin.

A victim is 70 times more likely to be killed by her abuser in the two weeks after she leaves than at any other time during the relationship. (Please note that this statistic does not apply to men as female abusers are less prone to physical violence and more prone to using verbal and emotional abuse and manipulation, except when it comes to child abuse.) During that time, fear, paranoia, and anxiety are kicked into overdrive. You find yourself looking over your shoulder constantly, afraid to walk down the street alone, don't like leaving the house, have heart palpitations every time you see a car similar to his, can't even *think* about sex because eventually you figure out that what he was doing was rape, and have all sorts of conditioned responses to triggers that won't go away for years to come. You don't have good relationships because you're too messed up to be level-headed, you may dabble in drugs or get fully addicted, you may become an alcoholic, your children may run and hide from any man who has even a single similarity to the abuser or raises his voice, your children may develop bedwetting problems or severe nightmares, and the list goes on and on.

It's definitely not over when you leave. It might *never* be over completely. The emotional fallout is overwhelming and heartbreaking. People don't usually think about that part, though.

Another thing people don't usually consider is that emotional and verbal abuse can be just as damaging as physical abuse, if not more so. There are some pieces contained here that address that, and this part actually really bothered me. Emotional scarring lasts much longer and requires a mental and emotional skill set to heal from that not everyone has access to.

The goal of an abuser is simple: to gain full control over his victim using scare tactics, manipulation, control, isolation, threats, and violence. The abuser is a monster who gets his kicks from turning his victims into mindless, unquestioning, and fearful followers.

As I went through this year's submissions, I was again faced with a barrage of familiar emotions, but this time I felt more disgust at knowing people like that are out there than anything else. Of course some of the pieces brought tears to my eyes; some of the scenes in this book are absolutely brutal and horrifying. I put the worst ones in the beginning of the book for one simple reason: to remind readers about the ugly reality of abuse before moving into the power of hope and the strength it takes for survivors to leave and speak out.

There is usually a long period of suffering and emotional turmoil, even suicidal thoughts and attempts, after someone leaves an abuser. If you have been away from your abuser for a while but are still struggling, you probably can't put your finger on it. You probably wonder why you aren't happy.

What helped to get me past that phase was a decision. Do I want to live like this, in fear of this asshole, for the rest of my life? Or do I want to rebuild my mind, body, and soul to be who I *want* to be? **As long as that fear is alive, his control over you will be as powerful as ever.**

To help you get there, take the advice of some of the authors offering encouragement and light in this book. It's a good idea to read books or watch movies that inspire you. For me, it was *The Secret, The Magic, Hero* (all by Rhonda Byrne), *Unlimited Power* by Anthony Robbins, and a number of other self-help and inspirational books. I also wrote obsessively in my journal for years, trying to unearth and dig through the remaining rubble in my heart and put it back together in a way that made sense.

Though there isn't a one-size-fits-all strategy for overcoming PTSD and all the baggage that comes with it, I do know it is manageable and you can still be the best version of yourself. Maybe even better, because now you're armed with the knowledge that **if you can leave an abuser who threatened your life on a constant basis and live to tell about it... you can do anything.**

When reading some of these stories and poems, I hope you'll remember that domestic violence, spousal rape, abuse, and the use of fear and control as a means to dictate lives are not pretty, romantic, or pleasant. Let this also serve as a disclaimer: there is adult language, graphic description, and violence within these pages. That is the nature of this particular beast. But even if it makes you uncomfortable... even if it makes you cringe, gives you chills, makes you cry, induces nausea, or pisses you off, I encourage you to read it and remember that people go through this each and every day, all over the world.

This collection is for those people. There is still hope hiding in the back of your heart. No one deserves to be abused and I hope that the strength portrayed in these pages seeps into you, whether you've left already or are still trapped.

I know you are strong. I believe in you. I hope you believe in yourself, too.

Honeymoon

Abuser behaviors:
Apologizes, makes amends, makes excuses, justifies violent behaviors, makes promises, blames drugs or alcohol, professes love.

Victim response:
Sets up counseling sessions, drops legal actions, forgiveness, returns or stays, hopeful, loving.

Tension

Abuser behaviors:
Name calling, accusations of unfaithfulness, criticism of clothing, weight, etc., nitpicking, engages victim into arguments, withholds affection, uses children as leverage, threatens to kill self or victim, other threats.

Victim response:
Self-blame, tries to reason, tries to calm, tries to satisfy, agrees, avoids, withdraws.

Violence

Abuser behaviors:
Demeans, verbally insults and abuses, hits, pushes, spits, pulls hair, restrains, throws things, sexually abuses or rapes, prevents police contact, harrasses and abuses children or pets, blames victim for the abuse.

Victim response:
Tries to protect self and children, tries to calm abuser, hides, fights back, gives in, may or may not call police, leaves.

www.SoulVomit.com

14

Things to Keep in Mind

Each piece within these pages has a purpose and was chosen for a reason. There are many different voices here with many different perspectives; some more blunt than others, some more artistic, and some will throw you for a loop. Hopefully all of them will inspire thought or shed light on the issue at hand.

If you or anyone you know is in a domestic violence situation and you're seeking help, please call the **National Domestic Violence Hotline** at **1–800–799–SAFE (7233)** or TTY 1–800–787–3224.

You may also seek help online at **www.TheHotline.org**.

On Fear

There's only one way to let go:

Stop holding on.

www.SoulVomit.com

Darkness

William McKnight

Rebecca's hand trembled as she tried to light another cigarette. Her cracked and bloody mouth hurt trying to hold the Marlboro between her swelling lips, but she needed the nicotine. *Nicotine and cheap Bourbon are the answer,* she thought. *The only answer.*

Cowering in the kitchen, she heard closet doors slam shut and the rumble of drawers being rummaged as Bobby ransacked the trailer looking for the rent money she'd hidden from him. Several minutes of yelling and beating hadn't compelled her to disclose the hiding place, and she'd be damned if she'd tell him now. Besides, the hard part was over, she knew. It always followed the same pattern. She'd hear Bobby's Harley rumble into the driveway and she'd hold her breath, listening for his boot-stomps up the creaky wooden stairs leading to the trailer. She could always tell when he was fucked up. Something in his balance, the timing of the stomps and creaks. Then, he'd pound on the door.

"Becky! Open the fuckin' door, bitch!" he'd yell.

And she always opened the fuckin' door. Sometimes little Jimmy would cry. Sometimes he'd stay in his room, sobbing quietly, waiting out the storm.

Tonight had been the same. Bobby had come in, drunk and fucked up on meth supplied by his biker buddies. He needed cash and knew that Becky would have the rent money stashed away. He beat the shit out of her, raped her once, and then, when he couldn't keep his erection, beat her again. Like it was *her* fault. But she'd refused to hand over the rent money. She and Jimmy needed a place to live more than Bobby needed more crank.

Rebecca put out her cigarette and lit another, waiting for Bobby's ransacking of the trailer to wind to a conclusion and for him to hit her again before jumping back onto his hog and rumbling away. She inhaled deeply and felt the calming effects of the nicotine begin to soothe her panic.

"I ain't askin' again, cunt!" Bobby yelled, stomping into the small kitchen.

He reeked of sweat and beer and the cat-urine odor of meth, and his eyes were filled with the insane rage of a madman. He hovered over her and glowered down from behind. His 300-pound frame was covered in greasy hair and ornate tattoos of devils, swastikas, and naked women on motorcycles.

"Please, Bobby," she implored. "Jimmy starts kindergarten next month and we gotta have a place to live, a permanent address. We just can't get evicted again, Bobby!"

She flinched as Bobby drove a callused fist into her eye socket, knocking her off her stool.

"Shut up!" he yelled. "Shut up about the fuckin' kid!"

Rebecca pulled herself up off the dirty linoleum floor and leaned back against the kitchen counter. Her left eye was swollen shut and tears clouded the vision in her right. But her ears were fine, and she heard the metallic clink of Bobby's .45 and felt the cold steel placed harshly against her hot temple.

"Please, Bobby!" she begged. "For God's sake!"

∞

Bobby hadn't slept in four days. He'd been on a run with the guys and had shot-up several hundred dollars' worth of crank. The veins in his tattooed arms were so used up that he had to mainline into the veins in his neck; a trick he'd learned in the joint.

Bobby's parole wasn't going very well. His P.O. was always on his ass to pass a urine test and get a job, but Bobby couldn't hold a job for more than a few days without getting fired for "anger problems." And urine tests? No way!

Bill and Ray were waiting at the clubhouse for Bobby's return with some cash, and he wasn't going to disappoint them. Rebecca, one of the mothers of one of his illegitimate kids, always stashed the rent money somewhere inside her trailer. She always used to fork it over after a little work-over with his fists and boots, and she'd always put out a little to calm him down. But this time….

Bobby pressed the .45 against her matted, blood-soaked hair and dropped the safety switch.

"Now, bitch. Gimme the fuckin' money. Now!"

Couldn't she see that he was serious?

She turned her good eye toward him, tears mixing with blood and sweat and trickling down her tired, frightened face.

"Bobby, please leave. Just get on your bike and—"

She never finished the sentence. Bobby heard a roar and felt the recoil in his hand as he watched blood and brains splatter against kitchen cabinets, and he saw her body go limp and crumple to the floor.

A small voice cried out behind him. "Mommy!" the voice said, and he whirled, leveling his gun at the small boy in the doorway.

∞

Relaxing, Officer Sean McInnis – they called him Mac – sat behind the wheel of his cruiser and half-listened to the radio traffic as the dispatcher called other officers to an assortment of incidents. Using the street light outside the Minit-Mart for illumination, he scratched out the basic facts from his last call onto an Incident Report Short-Form as he waited for his partner, Jim Noble, to return with their coffees. Mac could do that. He was a Senior Officer now and had already received his retirement orders. Next week, he'd be done with all this.

"Mary Beth says, 'Hey Mac,'" his partner said, approaching the cruiser with Styrofoam coffee cups in both hands. His white teeth flashed a smile made brighter by the contrast against his ebony skin and blue uniform.

"Thanks, Jim," Mac said, taking a cup from his partner's hand.

"Six Nora Two Four," the radio squawked. "Domestic call, shots fired."

Mac reached for the hand-mic as he put the car in drive.

"Six Nora Two Four, go."

"Domestic dispute at the Blue Moon Trailer Court, seven two oh one Glendale Drive. Space number one-twelve. Complainant advises screaming and shots fired."

"Received," Mac spoke into the mic, gunning the cruiser's engine forward. "We'll be ten-eleven from seventeen hundred and Columbia. Any cover units available?"

"Check and advise, at twenty-two thirty-two hours."

Jim buckled his seat belt for the high-speed approach.

"Let's boogie, man," he sang out.

Mac knew the streets of Portland very well, and the Blue Moon Trailer Court was a hot spot in town. Every cop knew the place.

"Six Nora Two Four," the radio spoke.

"Six Nora Two Four," Jim answered. With Mac driving Code three, lights and sirens, Jim would do the radio work.

"Your ten-three zero will be one Sam twelve from Saint Johns and Lombard."

"Ten four," Jim said, hanging up the hand-mic.

"Sounds like our cover unit's gonna be a North Precinct guy," Jim announced, hanging up the mic.

"North guy, huh? Saint Jay's and Lombard? That'll put him about ten minutes out. We'll stage and wait outside, if we can."

"Sho-nuf, Boss," Jim answered, way too cheery for a shots-fired call. But he had confidence in Mac's ability to get them in and out alive. Big Mac had a great reputation in the department. He was lucky to have been assigned to have him as his Field Training Officer.

The cruiser ran Code Three until they were four blocks away. Then, Mac killed the lights and sirens and went in slow and blacked-out.

∞

Bobby didn't think. He didn't reflect. He just pulled the trigger and watched the little boy's chest cavity rip apart as the small bundle collapsed onto the floor a few feet away from his mother's corpse. The little guy twitched and whimpered, gasping for air.

∞

Before he had closed the car door behind him, Mac heard the shot ring out.

"Mother of God," he muttered, in silent prayer.

Seeing the crowd of trailer-park neighbors gathering in the driveway and street, made dark by the great number of burnt out lights lining the rows of trailers, Mac turned to his partner.

"Call us, ten sixty, additional shots fired. And get us more cover. Code Three."

Jim nodded, clicked on his portable pack-set, and spoke quickly into the hand-mic clipped to his shirt. He advised the dispatcher of their arrival, the additional shot they'd heard, and he requested more cops, pronto, as Mac had ordered.

"Folks," Mac pushed the crowd back, "get the hell outta here. Get back! Do it! Do it, now!" he yelled.

Big Mac had a commanding presence. His 6'3" frame was intimidating enough, and his short-cropped hair and bushy mustache gave him a lumberjack appearance. The body armor he wore made him look positively herculean. The bystanders meekly retreated as Mac returned his attention to Trailer Space 112.

He scanned the area for clues to what he might face inside. He knew that he would have to enter; that he couldn't await the back-up units racing toward him, Code Three. Someone inside was probably dead or dying. Some innocent person, perhaps.

Mac noticed the Harley-Davidson parked in the driveway and the Nazi helmet hanging from the chopper's handlebars. He saw the dented, paint-chipped green station wagon with a child's car seat parked next to the Harley, and he saw the porch light flickering off and on, ready to burn out at any moment.

The North Precinct officer rolled up, the first of his cover units. The officer jumped out of his car and rushed toward Mac, gun drawn, but carried at the low-ready.

"What'cha got?" he panted.

"Multiple shots fired from inside one-twelve. Go to the back, contain the rear door. We'll enter through the front. Is your radio on tac-channel one?"

Most police agencies used a special tactical channel for building entries, in case the occupants were monitoring a Police Scanner inside. The cover-officer nodded and trotted back to the rear of the trailer.

Mac crossed himself and muttered a prayer.

"Protect us, Father," he whispered, drawing his .45 caliber Sig-Sauer P220 from the holster, "and help us to protect others. Amen."

Mac gripped the Sig-Sauer with both hands and, assuming a good stance, held the gun at the low-ready as he moved toward the front door. As the senior officer, he would be primary, or contact. Jim, his rookie partner, would be the cover officer, following Mac inside after he made the initial entry.

Barely breathing, both officers approached the trailer quietly. Mac stopped and listened, his ear cocked to an open window.

"Jimmy! Jimmy!" he heard a man's voice from inside, sobbing. "Jimmy, you dumb little fuck! It wasn't supposed to be like this! You dumb little fuck!" The man was obviously wracked with grief, and Mac estimated, ten or twelve feet away, somewhere inside the trailer.

Outside, the rickety wooden steps creaked as Mac slowly ascended, making his way to the front door. He stopped and crouched, waiting for Jim to get into position on the door knob side while he held the hinge side. Jim took his position and raised his own .40 caliber Glock from low-ready to aim as Mac reached his big, freckled hand up and banged on the front door.

"Police Department. Open the door! Police!"

They waited for ten or fifteen long seconds and then Mac pounded again.

"Open the door, now! Police!" Mac listened carefully but could hear nothing. The sound of the man sobbing had stopped and all that could be heard was the low background noise of a TV in some distant back room.

"Ready?" Mac whispered to his partner.

"Sho-nuf, Boss Man."

Mac tightened the grip on his Sig-Sauer, took a breath, and nodded. As contact officer, he'd be the first inside as Jim opened the door for him and covered from outside. Then, Mac would cover as Jim entered. The entry was the most dangerous part. At the Police Academy, they called it the "Funnel of Death" because officers are funneled through a narrow doorway and the doorway can quickly become a kill-zone for anyone laying in ambush.

∞

Bobby's heart pounded furiously in his chest. Driven by four days of shooting meth and the awareness that he'd just shot his own son and the kid's slut mother, Bobby was already wired tight when he heard the cops pounding on the door.

"Fuck!" he muttered, pushing away from his son's dying, twitching body and crawling behind a big, over-stuffed reclining chair to wait and think.

His mind raced as he tried to devise a solution to the mess, but he quickly realized that he was out of options. Then, he started to think again about prison. The confinement, the boredom, the brutality.

"I ain't goin' back to the fuckin' joint, man," he whispered to himself, checking the safety switch on his Colt .45. "No fuckin' way." Then, raising the muzzle toward the front door, he shouted, "Bring it on, pig mother-fuckers! Bring it on!"

∞

Mac nodded and Jim reached out and turned the door knob slowly, then pushed the door hard, forcing it back against its hinges as Mac dashed inside.

Inside, the trailer was engulfed in shadowy darkness. The only light came from the TV. But even in the dim TV light, Mac could see the little boy's crumpled body lying on the floor, clutching the hand of a woman's body, sprawled out in a pool of slippery blood on the floor leading to the kitchen. Mac felt Jim enter behind him and cut right, seeking the partial cover of a tattered sofa, scanning the room for signs of the shooter.

"We're inside," Jim whispered into the radio, informing the back door officer of their entry and continuing to scan for danger in the darkness.

But Mac's eyes were transfixed on the little boy. Mac couldn't shake his focus, couldn't break his attention from the bloody child on the floor. Mac walked toward the boy, his gun hand relaxing. It was almost like he was sleepwalking as he staggered toward the child. Mac had a little boy of his own at home, safe with his mother. Mac drew closer and closer until he could see the boy's face.

"He's alive," Mac whispered hoarsely. "The boy's alive!"

Mac's eyes met the boy's and he saw that the boy's mouth was moving. No sound came out, but his mouth formed words as he stared up at Mac. Blood dripped from his little mouth.

"Why, Daddy? Why?" the boy seemed to say. "Why, Daddy?"

Mac froze a moment and his gun-hand dropped to his side.

Behind him, Mac heard Jim yell loudly. From the corner of his eye, he saw a large, hairy form rise up from behind an over-stuffed chair. He saw the form, like in slow motion, pointing something at him.

Mac heard the explosion and saw the muzzle-flashes from behind the big chair, and he felt something hit him. He felt his body slam backward against the door frame. Life stopped for a brief moment and then went on, dream-like, in slow motion. He saw the bearded face and tattoo-covered arms of the fat guy with the gun. Strangely, he saw every detail of the gun and watched as, in slow motion, the slide rocked back and forth between muzzle-flashes and casings ejected from the ejection-port as round after round was fired into him. He felt sharp jolts hitting his ribs, between the panels in his armored vest, as a round ripped his face open. He tried in vain to whirl around and fire his Sig-Sauer back at the bearded man, but his body wouldn't move, wouldn't respond to his brain's commands.

In his periphery, Mac saw Jim move forward and heard the explosions booming from Jim's Glock as his rookie partner fired repeatedly into the hairy, tattooed fat man. He heard Jim yelling as he advanced on the shooter, but Jim's gunfire masked the sound of his own voice. He saw bullets tearing into the bearded face, splitting the man's head like a watermelon pelted by gravel, and saw the man flop face down onto the floor next to the big chair.

Mac stared at the dead man and saw the boy and the dead woman laying behind him, each laying in a pool of their own blood.

He felt the floor smack him in the ass and felt the weight of his Sig-Sauer go light as his numb arm dropped the gun onto the floor next to him. He leaned back, hearing the sound of waves, kind of a hollow, rushing sound, as his head lolled back and his eyes rolled. And… he felt something strange, something indescribable. He felt like… he felt like his spirit was being pulled, tugged really; tugged out of his mangled body.

"Sweet Jesus," he mumbled, as bloody bubbles sprang from his mouth.

And then, darkness.

Cream Soda

Joshua "Weck" Woeckener

When I was a kid,
it was all about
the cream soda.
The vanilla sweetness
reached its destination
and carbonation played
with my taste buds
as forever friends.

This was not completely why I consumed it.

I'd pass on
Coke, Dr. Pepper, Sprite,
knock-offs for the golden elixir.
Place the can's contents in a clear plastic cup;
you'll see.
It looks like beer.
A shallow reason,
but when you're five,
any inch closer
to manhood you can gain:
you take it.

The same reason I rocked my robe and slippers.
The same reason I sipped hot cocoa out of my Mickey Mouse
through-the-years mug.
The same reason I played little league through middle school.

The funny thing about emulation:
it's difficult to keep it selective.

Continuing this trend,
there are other traits
left for me to emulate.

The flavor of behavior
bringing me to tears
to the point I don't remember.
Well, who wants
to remember tears
crying timber
when inflicted by your father figure?

I figured father would bother
going out of his way
to keep his child's fears at bay;
not coming close to blows,
only stopping short due to a mother's presence.
Maybe I mouthed off,
employing sarcasm.
In my defense,
I was saying what you were portraying.

Buried memories became
hard-wired, land-mined
because I'd never know
when you might explode.

I was five foot six; the weight of a Benjamin.
You were five-ten; double mine; the size of a man.
Fortunately, I don't just appear one
nor explode on those too small to know
what's supposed to go down.

"This hurts me more than it hurts you,"
rolled off your lips each time

you displayed an act of love.
It's that trite act type that might find
its way in congregations;
weaving between pews
where lip service only serves lips
to ease the taste of iniquity.

It doesn't vanish.
Secrets surface surprisingly,
especially exactly
when we wish they wouldn't.

I'm not the only example.
Four want nothing to do with you,
two are too young to know better,
and one keeps connection,
not out of ignorance,
but out of hope for change.

I failed
in emulating you.
For that I'm thankful.
As I sip on cream soda,
tell me,
how does it taste?

Survivor of My Enemy

Marilyn Oakley

You sit there so cocky
Thinking you're so smart
Telling me to love you
And how to feel in my heart

You think you have one on me
You teacher, I a pupil in school
Your smile so sinister
Oh, but I *have* learned from you

You believe I'm still naive
And gullible to your words
And your threats of suicide
Please, don't be absurd

For I am wise to you
You pitiful little fool
You can't play with me
Your games so cold and cruel

So do what you must
But don't cross me
For I will not be a victim
Only a survivor of my enemy

A Coup in Chuckistan

Lee Smiley

In her mind, Susan thought of the little house as Chuckistan, the smallest sovereign nation in the world. Stretching from the cracked sidewalk at Hampton Drive to the back privacy fence, and from the side alley beside the house to the hedgerow separating it from the Spencer residence next door, Chuckistan stood unrecognized beyond its own borders, but that affected nothing that happened on that half acre. There, Charles Edward Funke – King Chuck to his wife and only subject – ruled with an iron fist, one he used as often as possible on Susan's face.

Sitting at the kitchen table, Susan slid her hand up the left side of her face to survey the damage from the previous night again. Her eye, swollen shut before she went to bed, was now almost fully open, although she could still feel the puffy ring of pain that yielded beneath her probing fingers. The cuts at the bridge of her nose and along the ridge of her cheekbone had scabbed over. The cut in her lip, however, was proving more of a problem and she could taste the familiar, coppery taste in her mouth. She continued to prod the tender spots, digging her fingers into the bruised flesh, the pain reminding her of how it had come to be that way. The pain fueled her anger which, in turn, fueled her resolve.

When she finally pulled her hand away, she touched the shotgun lying on the table before her, the cold steel a relief to her hot skin.

The phone on the wall rang and Susan jumped. She made no move to answer it, letting it ring and ring until the caller gave up and silence returned to the small kitchen. She had turned the answering machine off, afraid that even the pseudo-cheery chatter of a telemarketer might weaken her, that any influence from outside Chuckistan's borders might make her reconsider her decision.

Her hand closed around the gun, her fingers curling around the barrel until her knuckles whitened.

How did I ever let it get this far? Susan wondered. She pictured herself, 19 again, talking to the handsome student in her chemistry class. Even then there were signs, portents of their life together. His loud manner of speaking in a crowd, making sure that all eyes were on him, all ears hearing what he had to say. His overbearing but fragile ego. His demeaning attitude toward women. Even his anger, culminating in the senseless murder of an Erlenmeyer flask hurled against the cinder block wall after a failed experiment. All of it, everything that had stripped away Susan's identity, self-confidence, and happiness over the past ten years, was there from the very beginning, begging her to see it before she made a crucial mistake.

Now, too late to salvage the young woman she was and the dreams she had then, she just wanted to exact some revenge.

She could hear the cars passing the house on Hampton and, despite her self-promise to focus, wondered about the people driving them. Who were they? Susan imagined soccer moms on their way to pick up children from practice. Young couples, holding hands on their way to the grocery store. Weary, blue collar workers, their Wellington boots still caked with mud from the morning's rain, driving home, talking on cell phones to the wives they would see in a matter of minutes. She wondered if any of them stopping at the four-way at the corner bothered to look over the sidewalk, across the border into Chuckistan, perhaps sensing the revolution about to begin.

Her cell phone rang from the kitchen counter, but this time she did not flinch. She turned to the small, outdated gadget, one of Chuck's few concessions in the area of communication with the outside. The unit lay face down so she could not see the caller ID and she almost rose to see who it was before her hand, still clutching the shotgun, held her back like a chain. If someone was calling her cell, it must be family, someone concerned that she had not spoken with them in a few days. Susan had broken off diplomatic ties with everyone she cared about so she could build up to the task at hand and only hoped that now, at her moment of resolution, none of them decided to check in on her in person.

Still, part of her wondered who out there cared enough to call. Sometimes, locked inside the house for days, her phone privileges taken away by His Majesty, she tended to think the rest of the world had become nothing more than a pleasant fantasy to prop up her false hopes, a fallacy her battered ego would not let go. Was it her mother, that Secretary of Stateliness, who knew but would never acknowledge that her daughter had married an abusive megalomaniac? Was it her father, the Minister of Commercials, sitting in front of the television all day and night to avoid dealing with the real world where daughters do, in fact, get pummeled by their husbands? Could it even be her older sister, from the Department of Interior Design, too wrapped up in her business to have a husband or time to discuss her sister's problems?

It didn't matter. None of them, no one she thought actually cared about her, wanted to hear where her frequent bruises came from or why she wasn't allowed outside for days on end. Abuse was something that happened to other people, people her father saw on the news, not to someone who had lived under their same roof for nearly two decades. She took some grim satisfaction in the idea that the first her father might hear about what she was going to do would likely be on the ten o'clock news.

Finally, the cell phone stopped ringing, giving one final chirp to indicate that whoever had called had left a voice mail.

Good for them, Susan thought. *Voice mail. One more thing I won't have to—*

Her mind snapped back into focus as the familiar sound of the garage door opening to allow King Chuck's royal carriage, a newish Mercedes, to pull in next to her rust-spotted Ford, the only set of keys to which hung from His Royal Highness's keychain. As the opener raised then lowered the segmented door, her heart rate sped up, increasing with every pop and whine from the machine as it heralded the lord of the manor.

The interior door to the garage opened and King Chuck entered, dropping his briefcase on the floor beside the refrigerator as he did every day. His tie half undone around his neck, the tailored jacket hung loose on his shoulders, he ignored his wife, sitting at the kitchen table a few feet away, and tossed his keys into the plastic basket she had set near the door for him. He opened the fridge and rummaged inside, as he always did when he came home to his kingdom, and pulled out a Budweiser.

"Where's dinner?" he asked her, twisting the bottle cap off and taking a long pull.

Susan did not answer, afraid that any words that passed her mouth now might give her away.

King Chuck stood at the open refrigerator and finished his beer in three long swallows before grabbing another from inside.

"I asked you," he said, still not looking at her, "where is my dinner?"

Susan felt her body trembling all over, all except for the hand that held the shotgun as though she hung from it over some great precipice. For her, it was no longer a matter of not wanting to answer her husband's question; it was an impossibility.

"What the fuck is wrong—?" Chuck began. Then he turned and looked at his wife and the shotgun in her hand. No part of him moved except for his eyes, which narrowed in that dangerous way Susan had seen a thousand times since she had agreed to be his queen. Several seconds passed before anything else happened, then Chuck raised the beer bottle to his lips and took a sip.

When he lowered the bottle again, King Chuck was smiling.

He stepped back and closed the refrigerator, never taking his eyes off her. The beer came up again for another lengthy pull, and he stepped to the kitchen table, taking the seat opposite his wife, the smile never faltering. Setting the bottle on the table, he leaned back in the chair and raised his arms slowly, interlocking his fingers at the back of his head.

"What the hell do you think you're doing?" he asked. His tone was that of an adult speaking to a toddler, a patronizing, snide voice that matched his smug grin. "You going to shoot me, Suzie?"

Susan tried to answer, opened her mouth and felt the word form, the air pumping up from her lungs and taking shape in her throat before dying, unceremoniously, on her lips. A tiny squeak and a short nod were all she could manage.

Chuck watched her over the Budweiser, assessing her, peering at her as though he were examining some x-ray of her. Looking for a spine that he was sure he had permanently removed.

"I bet that thing's not even loaded." His hand slid across the table, snake-like, reaching for the shotgun.

Susan stood, knocking her chair over in her haste, yanking the shotgun off the table out from beneath his descending fingers. She gripped it in her hands like a child who had wandered briefly from his mother's sight, caressing it as though it had hair to tousle. Beneath her fingers, she found comfort in the tactile sensations it gave her; it was cold, hard, deadly. Just as she now needed to be cold, hard, deadly.

Chuck stared at her when she pulled the gun away from him, anger flaring for just a moment in his green eyes before washing away in a new tide of amusement. "See, I didn't think so. What are you going to do with an unloaded gun? Hit me over the head with it?"

"Itsloaded." The two words came out as one. Susan could not remember the last time she had dared correct King Chuck, and the suddenness of it both thrilled and terrified her.

Chuck's eyebrows raised, lifted perhaps by the heat that again flared in his eyes. He gave her that penetrating stare again, looking her up and down, searching for something he may have missed in his initial spinal examination. Picking up the beer bottle, he drained the remaining liquid from it and, with a blinding motion, threw it against the refrigerator.

"Do you think you're going to scare me, you fucking bitch?" King Chuck roared at his subject. He stood up, knocking his own chair over and sliding the table several inches toward Susan with a staccato yowl. "You think I'm scared of you, cunt? You think you're going to wave a fucking gun in my face and you're not going to pay for it?"

Susan raised the gun barrel level with his face, although her shaking hands made it difficult for her to hold it steady. She kept her finger off the trigger, still unwilling to commit the act to chance. *If I'm going to murder him,* she thought through her fear, *I want to mean it.*

Chuck pushed the table again and this time it collided with her thighs, not hard enough to knock her over or even send her off balance, but enough to leave her with new bruises to match those on her face and arms.

She slid her finger down over the trigger. The move was automatic, more an act of instinct than one of thought.

"I give you everything," Chuck continued to scream, waving his hands at the small house surrounding them. "I give you food and a roof over your goddamn head and a fucking phone and... and here you are, you ungrateful cunt, waving a goddamn gun at me. You motherfucking, goddamn ungrateful whor—"

Words have weight. Mass. Every goddamn, every fucking, every cunt and bitch and whore he had called her for a decade all collected on Susan's finger, gathered there like flies on a corpse, pressing her finger onto the trigger. She raised the gun to eye level, feeling the stock against the painful skin of her face.

Susan did not hear the gun when it went off. The sound of the twin barrels releasing their loads combined with the verbal assault supplanted it to become one great howl of rage, first raised by her husband, then answered by her. Still, she heard none of it. None of her fury exploding out the long, steel shafts to erase her husband's.

What Susan heard was tinkling. As the shotgun blasted King Chuck's face through — then out the back of — his skull, over the ripping of the debris into the drywall, the living room furniture, and the front bay window, over even the splatter of her husband's flesh, bones, and brains as they sprayed in a reddish cone out behind him, Susan heard the tinkling of the china in the cabinets, shaken by the resonance of the gun or, she thought later, the resonance of how she had used it. The china continued to rattle even a few seconds after the late King Chuck's remains collapsed to the floor, like tiny applause, the ghosts of her past, her lost dreams, saluting this act of savage bravery.

The gun was no longer cold. Beneath her white fingers, the metal blazed, still flushed from its use. She dropped it, feeling betrayed by the heat. It clattered to the floor, chipping one square of the expensive tile, and she kicked it away from her. The gun came to rest against the Bostonian loafer on Chuck's left foot.

She willed herself to look at him. Lying in a white-flecked pool of blood, the thick red liquid filling in the grouted lines between the tiles, the body lay still. Examining the bloody mass that had been her husband's face with a calm detachment that surprised her, she would have said he was unrecognizable, except that he wasn't. This horrific, dead monster lying on her kitchen floor, its blood pooling on the white ceramic, was the real King Chuck. This creature, wearing its violence like a

Halloween mask, was the husband she had lived with for the past ten years.

He was dead.

She was free.

Later, Susan never remembered falling to her knees. She lay on the floor sobbing while time stopped around her, allowing her to release the emotion she had been saving for so long. Night fell as she cried and soon the only illumination in the room was from the street light that lit the alley beside the house, diving in at a slant as though afraid to bear witness to what she had done. In some remote region of her mind where she maintained some tenuous connection with the real world, she heard her cell phone ring and stop. Ring and stop. She could not say if the rings came together or were from separate calls. A maelstrom of grief and fear and relief had dragged her down beneath the surface of her life where she cared about things such as phone calls. At some point, exhausted, she slept.

It was the smell that finally brought her around. As the blood on the floor began to congeal, the metallic scent of it, so common from her own body, brought her around to wakefulness. For a fearful moment, she was sure she had dreamed it all and that King Chuck was there, standing over her, ready to issue another royal proclamation of the fist. Then, she saw the shotgun and, beyond that, the Bostonian, its toe pointed upward.

She almost slipped down again, almost waded into those waters of relief and forgetfulness, but the smell of blood could still motivate her. She got to her feet, taking in the scene anew in the diminished light. She did not bother to turn on the lights. Better to remember it this way.

Her cell phone buzzed again on the counter and this time, her hand steady, she picked it up.

Dad, the display read. She flipped it open.

"Daddy," she said. Her voice was small, childlike. "Come get me, Daddy. I've done a bad thing."

She flipped the phone shut, reopened it, turned it off, and dropped it onto the floor. She righted her fallen chair and moved the table back into place. Then, she sat down…

… and waited.

Young Brides

Katie Rendon Kahn

A young bride worries about
where her husband is at night.
She calls obsessively,
drives past suspected houses
and bars. She enlists friends
to help search for evidence,
interrogates his coworkers,
and frequently embarrasses
them both.

Eventually she'll accept
that he'll stumble in
when the bars close,
smelling like Jack Daniels
and pussy.
She'll be grateful
that is wasn't her
this time.

Third Floor

Lee Ann Perez

I arrive home on a warm summer's night after a friend's birthday party. As I lock the car door, something slams into the side of my head; the pain is excruciating and I fall to the ground. As I pull myself up, an unfamiliar man is standing over me. His black eyes are wild, filled with hatred and rage. He grabs my hair and arm while dragging me to the stairs of my apartment. I muster a piercing cry for help and cannot get out of his strong grip. My body is being dragged over the gnawing concrete that rips the shoes from my feet. I am in shock and disbelief that this is happening to me.

He holds me tight and demands that I open the apartment door; fearing for my life, I follow his orders. Once inside, I break loose from his grip and sprint across the living room into the kitchen in hopes of dialing 911, but he reaches the phone before I do and rips it out of the wall. His eyes are on fire as he screams, "You fucking bitch! You need to learn a lesson! Why do you do this to me?" and proceeds to strike my face with his fist. He pushes me through the living room and into my bedroom where he bites my back over and over again like a mad hyena, finally throwing me down on the bed and walking out of the room. The horror coupled with fear paralyzes me and I'm terrified to speak, terrified to move, and terrified to attempt an escape.

As I sit motionless on my bed, I am blinded by the white paint that covers each wall surrounding me. No paintings or pictures hang on these unpadded walls. My apartment has been transformed into a solitary confinement cell in the psychiatric ward, and I am ensnared with its patient.

A few minutes pass and the man returns, towering over me, holding a handgun and completely naked. He opens the cylinder and explains there is only a single bullet awaiting discharge. The cylinder is closed and the barrel is jammed to my head; he pulls the trigger and the gun does not fire. His demonic howling increases and reverberates off the barren walls as he continues to spew, "You fucking bitch! You need to learn a lesson!" But this soon transforms into a revolting sob.

The naked intruder stands before me, crying. I realize he is now flirting with his own death and turns the gun on himself. The gun dances back and forth from his head to his mouth. As I watch in horror, imagining his brains and blood splattered on the wall, I am not scared; I want to see him pull the fucking trigger. For a brief moment, my hatred for this human being wants to see his splatter cover these walls.

I'm not sure if he will turn the gun on me again, so in a sickening, sweet, high-pitched toddler's voice I say, "Don't cry, you are a good person who is loved by your family and friends. You don't want to do this. Put the gun down and everything will be all right." The naked man calms down and returns to the living room.

I become deaf to my surroundings and hear only the pounding of my heart. Movements are in slow motion, but my mind is rapidly planning an escape. Slowly I walk out of the bedroom and into the living room. All of the lights have been turned off and his silhouette is lying on my couch, which is next to the front door. The tall white walls reflect the moon's light filtering through the sliding glass door and surrounding bay windows, making it possible to see his pallid skin and the shimmering metal of the gun.

I plead, while speaking in that toddler's tone, for permission to go outside on the back deck, and he agrees. From the living room, through the glass doors I hover, ever so cautiously onto the deck and start praying, for tonight I will die. In preparation for my arrival at his gates, I make amends with my Lord and my fear of pain is lifted.

My prayer gives me a sense of courage to escape and I'll do so by jumping out the third story bedroom window. Warily, I walk past his pale silhouette, enter my bedroom, and notice that I am still holding my car keys from when I locked the car doors. I do not fear leaping from the third story window, but realize that the mini-blinds squeak when lifted. The only thing stopping me from flying out that window is the noise, because if he hears that he will come running for me. This leaves the front door as my only alternative to escape.

Barefoot and clutching my car keys, I hold my breath while tiptoeing ever so lightly toward the front door. I gradually reach for the door knob and prepare myself to run down the stairs. I turn my head to see the home invader asleep on the couch. The knob turns and the door opens. Like a gazelle running away from a cheetah, I jump and soar high over the steps. My heart hammering and thoughts racing, I do not stop. This is survival and I am the prey; it's escape or perish. I make it to my car alive and drive as fast as I can, breaking all speed limits en route to my parents'. I beat on their door until it opens and dash to the phone to immediately call the police.

Upon the officers' arrival I give a statement and they write a report of the incident. They proceed to take photographs of the bite marks on my back and my distended, black-and-blue face. In order for the police to make an arrest I need to identify the suspect. This entails driving back to the scene; my fear returns and I tremble as I hand them my apartment keys. I tell them I cannot go anywhere near that building, so I wait alone in the overpowering darkness, two apartment buildings away.

According to the police report filed later, the police entered the apartment to find my coffee table blocking the front door and a large kitchen knife lying upon it. When they entered the bedroom, the naked man was sitting on my bed, holding the gun, and live ammunition was scattered on the mattress. They told him three times to drop the gun and he refused. On the fourth order to drop the gun, the man did so but resisted arrest.

The police were ready to shoot him, but the man finally surrendered. The officers arrested the criminal and booked him into the county jail, where he awaited trial for two counts of assault in the second degree with the deadly weapon enhancement and two counts of assault in the fourth degree. The next day, I filed divorce papers against this assailant, this stranger, and this "wife beater..." my husband.

I was 24 years old when I married this man. We dated a few months before he asked my hand in marriage, and during this time, he showed no signs of violence. I should have dated him longer in order to get to know him, a mistake that almost cost me my life. At any rate, we were only married three months prior to this incident.

The local newspaper snatched up the tragic story and printed it. I am unsure why they thought it necessary to include my name in their article, but they did, and in doing so they compounded the shame and embarrassment I, a victim of domestic abuse, already felt. A few women who had previously dated this man contacted me and told me they, too, were abused by him and gave me their condolences. Through my anguish, anger, and pain, I recovered, and as a result, moved on with my life.

Monsters

Debbie Lechtman

I.

When I was five and six and seven, I asked my parents about monsters. "They don't exist," Dad said every time, his eyes glued to the television screen; the football game was on and it was important.

"I think they do," I always whispered, because I thought they did.

"Don't be ridiculous," Mom yelled from the kitchen. Maybe she was scrubbing the dishes or putting a pie in the oven. What she did changed, but the answer was the same: ridiculous. Don't be ridiculous.

Later I found out the truth. My parents had lied to me, or maybe they were just ignorant and wrong. "I think they do," I'd said, and I'd been right from the start.

II.

When he is angry, he is like a hurricane. I can see his thoughts spinning and spinning and spinning, and if I'm not careful enough, they spin inside me, too, in my gut and in my heart, so I have to close my eyes tight and pretend I'm somewhere else. I think about Dad and his football, about Mom and her pies.

III.

The time I got brave I said if he hurt me again I'd go to the police. So he said, "Go right ahead, slut," and he hurt me again anyway.

He grabbed me by the ponytail and pulled down on my hair so my face turned up to the sky like a seesaw. It didn't hurt

45

that bad where he pulled – maybe it stung a little like I'd ran into a bee – but then my knees buckled and the back of my head landed with a *wham* on the coffee table, and for the next few minutes, all I could see were the stars, but not real stars. Fake stars, like the stars inside my head.

He hurt me stupid, I joked to myself over the next few days whenever my heart tried to get upset. Because joking about it was better than crying.

Anyway, then I rubbed my eyes hard so he couldn't see my tears and he said, "What are you going to do about it? You going to the *po-lice*?"

He said police like it was the funniest thing he ever heard.

I shook my head no, I'm not going to the police, but of course he already knew that.

"What are you going to do about it?" he asked.

Not a damn thing. Not a damn thing.

IV.

One time I tried to tell Mom about it, but then I chickened out because she'd hate him, and what would I do if she hated him? I couldn't stand that, Mom hating him.

Anyway, telling Dad was out of the question because football was on again.

V.

When we broke up, I remembered what happened three years before, when I said no but he had sex with me anyway.

I thought then it wasn't rape, because he was my boyfriend so of course he thought that gave him permission.

The truth is that it didn't. Three years later I had to remind myself that it didn't.

IV.

When you are single you have a lot of time to just do things, like meet up with your girlfriends for drinks at the bar.

"He can't have been that bad," my friend said over her fuzzy pink cocktail. It looked pretty girlish, but to me she seemed good and drunk already. I felt tipsy myself, my brain wobbly and my feet tingly and light. She thought she knew me because in college we'd talked about boys.

"He was pretty bad," I said, my chest swelling with irritation. Of course I felt defensive. "He was actually abusive."

I thought maybe she'd be shocked when I said that, but instead she flicked her wrist in the air like, *whatever*. "Sweetie, if he'd been abusive, I'd know about it. If he'd been abusive, you would've told me."

Watermark

Andrea Barton

I don't wear scarves
anymore:
somewhere between
my clavicle and my throat
is my limit.
It is tender skin,
sensitive to the touch
of collars, lips, fingers, arms.
Sometimes my long hair
gets wrapped around it
in a good wind
or while swimming sideways.
That makes me whip it off
quickly because it reminds me
of when I couldn't whip
your lips
your fingers
your arm
off my throat
and I thought
I would die,
each time
a different way.

Little Creatures

Jaclyn Crombie

It smells damp under here. There are little creatures nesting in the heat. Multi-colored bugs scuttle across my arms as I lie still. Today is the fourth day that I have hidden at six o'clock. Yesterday I hid in Mum's old suitcase in the shed. When He came to find me, I heard Him and ran. I made it all the way to the neighbor's fence line before He caught me and brought me home. Every day is worse. But this time—

I won't move, I won't run. He'll never find me here. I've made myself a little coffin under the house and only God knows I'm here. I'm going to stay here and pray that God will come and take me away. Please, God, don't make me hide for one more day.

The dogs have stopped barking, so I know He must be coming. They go each day to hide in the woodpile when they hear His Ute. That's how I got this idea.

I feel my arms beginning to shake. The heat under this house is suffocating. My legs are twitching with irritation at the bugs making a home there. I wonder who will get me first: Him, God, or the worms.

As the Ute gets closer, the sound of grinding metal is winding down and I hear it rattle to a stop. The car door shuts with a *slam!* that sends a jolt through me, like a boot of electricity. I screw up my face against the stench of rotting meat as He walks closer.

The old house shudders as His chunky, brown, bloodstained boots *thump, thump, thump* up the wooden front steps. With each *thump*, crusty flakes of mud sprinkle down on me from the underbelly of the house. My limbs are shaking, disrupting the little colonies working on them.

I am imagining what He will find inside the house. I can see clearly in my mind the ripped and faded orange carpet in the hall that He must be walking over. I hear Him thumping His big feet down towards the kitchen and I quake, knowing every speck of dirt on the floorboards and muck on the old hardwood benches.

This is where He will find Her. It is where I left Her, 'asleep,' sprawled over the kitchen floor. Two saucepans sit on the bench top. Another has fallen with a loud clatter to the floor, spilling cold water all over Her hair, leaving potatoes rolling near Her head and creating wet patterns on the floor.

I won't see tonight whether He picks Her up and carries Her tenderly to bed, or drags Her by the hair into a cold shower, only to half-drown Her into waking before beating Her again into 'sleep.' I won't see if He uses His fist or the belt, or tries to finish off the job She started with the bottle. And I won't hear it, either.

I am pressing my ears shut so hard that I think my fingers might break. I am squeezing my eyes closed tight. I won't know when it starts, or when it's over. I pray I won't know when He's coming for me.

I am wrong. I hear everything. I am pressed to the ground on my belly while the house is shuddering above me, His footsteps slamming into the floor.

She is not asleep anymore. Her screams are leaking through the cracks. Her heels are kicking near my head, trying to punish me for leaving Her like this. All at once a million bugs are on me, urging me to leave my hiding place. I will run to Her, I will save Her. I feel urgent in my muscles, in my skin. I will take a piece of wood from the pile, I will run in screaming, "Mummy, Mummy!" and I will beat Him until He hurts like Her and me.

I am trapped here. I am fear. He cannot hear me because He has Her, and She is screaming, but I press my sobbing face into the ground, stifling my cries, "Mummy, Mummy…."

Glass breaks and She is not screaming anymore. There is no more noise, no sounds of struggle. I feel like there are worms in my throat that I can't swallow. I slowly let the thoughts trickle into my mind like tears... has He killed Her? Is She dead?

What if She is dead? I start to cry like a baby. I don't want to cry. I tell myself not to and press my hands firmly over my mouth. She wasn't really my mother. She wasn't the way real mothers are. She didn't cuddle or kiss me. She didn't dress me or take me to school.

She didn't take care of me.

"You're better off without Her," I tell myself in an angry way. "She never loved you anyway."

The front door goes *slam!* and I jump backwards in fright as those big, bloodstained boots stomp back down the stairs. He forces a loud roar from His mouth that sounds like, "Ellen!" Through the gaps in the slats around the bottom of the house, I can see His face. He looks like a monster, with red eyes popping out, purple face, and veins near to bursting in His neck.

"Ellen!" He yells again. He is going with angry steps to look for me in the shed, where I hid yesterday. I am watching the shed door, waiting for Him to come back out. My heart is beating hard in my chest because I know He will find me eventually. He always does.

I am scared without my mother, even though She would never save me. I always hoped things would change, and one day She would love me and take me away from here. I felt like maybe if I thought it hard enough, it would be true. It always made me less scared, to keep that hope deep down inside. But if He finds me this time, the only person He'll have left to beat on is me.

It isn't long before He returns. He stands with His arms crossed tightly across His chest, staring with a narrow gaze and tight lips as He turns slowly, examining the yard. His eyes fix on the woodpile, and it looks to me like He's making plans.

He walks toward the woodpile, twigs cracking under his boots with every step. He is calling the dogs to Him in a hard voice, but they won't come. He whistles through his fingers, but they won't come. He spots one cowering on the ground behind a stack of wood.

"Get up! Find her, you lazy mutt!" He yells.

The dog only moves to shrink closer to the ground. They aren't dogs for hunting, they're just mongrels and they've never been trained. I should be glad for this, but I feel my heart hurting for the poor ugly dog that can't understand Him. Its face is scared and sad, almost begging, I think. I have been like that.

He is in a temper, like my mother would say, and He throws a piece of wood hard at the dog's head. He doesn't hit it – He's a bad shot when He's mad – and the dog dodges quickly, racing off across the yard toward the house.

He won't let it get away now, I know. He's said so many times before that He won't be beaten by some mutt… or some bitch… or some brat. He catches it trying to squeeze under the house, and its head is close to me when His hand reaches in and heaves it out by the collar. The dog whines and scratches in fear, clawing under the house. I slither slowly backwards on my belly. He is so close that I can see every blood stain on his overalls.

He heaves at the dog's collar, trying to pull it back. He gives one hard yank, but it won't move. I can see He is going to crack and I brace myself, but He doesn't. He stops yanking on the dog's collar and says softly, "What is it, boy? What you got?" I slide further backwards, slowly and silently. He lowers His head to look at me and I freeze.

I am squished back against a pillar in the darkness. I am not moving, not a single hair. I am not even breathing. I feel His eyes running over me, I feel Him trying to see in the dusk light.

The dog is still struggling in His grip. I am so frightened that the dog will find me out. I can't be caught. I have stayed out too long, and He will kill me, like maybe He has killed my mother.

I can't stay like this, God! I can't stay like this! I must move, I must cough, I must breathe!

He will find me, and He will hurt me again. Please God, save me! Please God, if She is alive, make *Her* save me!

I think of the last beating that would not end, and Her standing there watching with Her cigarette and bottle. I don't want more to come. I am staring at his eyes when the crying comes and overtakes me with violent trembling. I am not brave anymore. I can't stop it. My mouth opens to scream—

An incredible *crash!* shakes the house above me, and all the air leaves me. I can hear banging and cursing from inside the house. It sounds like Her. She is alive!

The dog yelps and struggles hard against His grip, knocking Him down as it breaks away and runs back to hide in the woodpile. He gives an angry roar and runs after it. He ties the dog to a tree and hits it for knocking Him down. I cover my ears and my eyes and try not to hear it squeal.

He is yelling as He approaches the house again, and I open my eyes and ears to see Him running up the front steps shouting, "Moira!" I shudder and sob with relief at not being found, but I am careful not to let a single sound get away from me. I hear stumbling around inside, and then running feet, and a door slams.

"Open the door, Moira!" He yells, and I hear Him pounding on it.

"Get away from me!" She screams.

I cannot hear what they are saying after that, only that they are roaring at each other. I am weeping, and my face feels soggy from tears.

∞

It has finally gotten dark. They have finally stopped yelling. I heard Him stomp into the lounge room, and the telly is blaring now.

It has become cold under here. My fingers are numb. The wind blows under the house and straight through my little cotton dress. Critters are crawling over me again, and it scares me in the dark.

I push out from underneath the house, wriggling and squirming. It scrapes all down my back and rips my dress, but I feel free. The air is softer out here, and the grass feels sweet on my feet. I might make it now, if I leave.

I run on tiptoe to the gate and grasp at the latch. My throat is jumping wildly. I think I might do it. Can I leave Her? What will happen if I go? I turn and see the light on in Her room. I feel bad; She is alone.

I stand at the gate and stare out at the dark. I am trembling, almost worse than before. I don't know what is out there. At least here I know.

He will be sleeping now, I tell myself. *He won't hurt you. He will be collapsed in front of the telly with his beer. He wouldn't hurt you, anyway, if you wouldn't run away,* I reason.

Tomorrow, I think. *Tomorrow I will try harder.*

My feet are taking me back toward the house. I am cold and hungry, and we are miles from anywhere. I will freeze on the highway if I go.

I climb the wooden steps and they creak. I push the front door open and feel the raggedy orange carpet under my feet. *He won't hurt you now,* I tell myself again. *He can't hurt you now.*

My chest tightens as I step into the lounge room.

"Daddy?"

Between the Lines

Katie Rendon Kahn

Secrets rest on split lips, spill from forced smiles that want to
whisper, but
       can't
Her burdens are barriers, blocking her from reaching out to
       you
and she wonders if people can
       read
the warning signs. She's caught
       between
nowhere to run and no one to turn to, swerving across
       the lines,
and she wonders:
       can't you read between the lines?

Set Me Free

Jennifer-Crystal Johnson

Being me
in a world full of you
is the hardest thing
I've had to do.

Leaving you
so that I can be me
was hard as well,
but will set me free.

www.SoulVomit.com

Penumbra

Nicholas P. Anthony

The girl was about 14 and barefoot. She stood in the shallows of the lake dressed only in a cross necklace and a white nightgown that was torn along one shoulder. The lake's water was cold and lapped gently against her ankles. Beneath her, the rocks felt smooth and hard as they pressed up against the soles of her feet.

The reflection of the moon shimmered on the surface of the lake. Its silver crescent appeared to dance atop the line of trees that stood reflected behind her, and the stars around it were few and covered by the occasional cloud. Behind the trees was a mountain and behind the mountain was a town, but the town could not be seen from the lake.

She waded further into the water. It was still cold, but her feet were beginning to numb. The water was soon at her knees and the bottom of her gown clung to her legs and made it difficult to take each step. The girl carefully untied the gown and tilted her shoulder, allowing it to slide off of her thin frame. Behind her, the gown rocked up and down in the shallows, its sash spindling away from it like a recently cut umbilical cord. It floated there for a moment before submerging beneath the waves.

The girl was naked and the water was now up to her thighs. Her skin was pale and mottled, resembling an abstract painting splashed here and there with blues and purples and yellows and greens. As she walked, her fingertips traced patterns on the surface of the lake that caused ripples to trail in her wake.

The water was at her waist when she heard the car. She heard the labored breathing of the engine and the sound of the tires as they ground over the pebbles on the beach. Headlights reflected off the lake's surface and illuminated the girl in pale fluorescence.

A car door opened and closed, and a man walked over to the lake's edge.

"Where are you going?" the man called. His voice was soft and his speech slurred, but his words still carried across the water.

"Away," the girl said.

"Away? Away where?"

The girl started to shiver.

"For God's sake, you're not wearing anything. It's freezing out."

"It'll get warmer."

"Why don't you come back? There's a fire going. We'll wrap you in a blanket and it'll be ok."

"It'll be ok."

"Yes. Come back home."

The girl took a few more steps into the lake. The water licked the bottom of her belly button.

"Are you insane? You're going to catch pneumonia."

"Not this time."

"I'll call the police."

The man began to pace back and forth. The pebbles crunched beneath his boots.

"I have my faults, I know, but I don't meant to... you know I don't mean...." the pacing stopped and the man looked up at the girl expectantly. "I love you, baby; I love you so much."

She paused and felt the current rock her body back and forth.

"Jesus, Helen. What do you want me to do? What do you want me to say? Do you want me to beg?"

She began to walk.

"Helen, please. Don't... don't do this."

She took another step. Her foot slipped on a rock and twisted, causing her to stumble and submerge beneath the water. She resurfaced moments later. Breathing calmly. The water trickled from her hair and down her breasts, collecting at the tips of each nipple until the droplets grew too heavy and fell.

"Helen?"

She began to wade once more into the lake.

"For Christ's sake, I'm sorry. Helen. I'm sorry!"

The water was almost to her breasts.

"Fuck this. Fuck this, fuck this, fuck this, fuck this."

The man kicked off his boots and stripped down to his boxers. He danced there on the shore for a minute, shaking the life into his limbs before running into the frigid, black waters of the lake.

The water was to her shoulders when the man reached her. He grabbed her gently and threw her over his shoulder. She hung there. Her wet hair draped in front of her face like yellow curtains. The man began to wade through the water, back to the shore and to his car. The girl never moved or made a sound. The water trickled down her cheeks.

Alone Again

Maxine Moncrieffe

As I sit in this world all alone
With no one to call my own…
Can't do it, can't be strong,
Wondering what it is I did wrong.
Destined to unhappiness, failure, and pain;
No matter what I do, it's all in vain.

No one cares, nothing to dream of…
None to give or receive this love.
Why am I here? What is there to gain?
Living this life has been such a strain.

Treated like trash, no one there…
Searching fruitlessly for someone, *anyone* to care.
Life of hell, no reason why;
Wishing and hoping I could just lay down and die….

Perfect Grave

Jessica Drummond

They started digging.

See, at first it was just one of the miniature men in a boy's disguise; he originally picked up a twig and started to dig, and when his stick broke he merely grabbed a larger one. He poked and prodded at the dirt and the grime and revealed a layer of clay, and even though his makeshift tools continually snapped, he just kept coming back with larger and larger sticks. One by one the rest of them followed suit, and they all had their fill of unearthing the ground and their hole grew to sizeable proportions.

They didn't know what they were digging for.

There were five of them. Four of these were adolescent boys, and one pubescent, loud, and colorful girl. She could hold her own and theirs. The forest was one of the magical places that they all escaped to. They discovered their hiding place in late summer and retreated faithfully each and every day after school. In the autumn the rain started to fall and their hole, now six feet deep, filled with water. She was the first to jump in it, and the green food coloring from her braids soaked upon her skin and made her look like a swamp monster as it mixed with the black she used to outline her eyes, and the other four all glimpsed touches of black and green permanently decorating her skin that wasn't going to wash off.

She was their little sister, their mascot, their love affair, their paramour, developing in front of them and so oblivious. Any of these boys could have had her at any moment. But for now, they just watched the colors she dripped as she jumped in the hole they had spent so long digging. And when she was done, they hoisted her out and gave her a towel and some hot chocolate.

They taught her how to smoke pot. How to really get high, inhale properly, hold it in, let it out, and that coughing is good. The first few times she didn't speak much, just stared at spider webs in silent wonder and listened to the birds sing their songs. They were content to just watch her fascination and the look in her eyes that made them think that she was at some sort of peace.

The snow came and laid the ground to rest and covered it with a soft blanket, freezing the entire world underneath them and nothing in their hole would budge. If they brushed away the frozen flakes, they found a frozen lake that lay at their feet, but nobody dared jump into the hole this time. They surrounded it and dangled their feet inside while passing around pipes, joints, or if brave, a bong. She was now always the first to pack a bowl. They noticed the black around her eyes looking heavier and more thickly-lined. She was always wiping at her eyes and smearing it, but the black never went anywhere.

Eventually the cold got to them and they would head into the basement of one of their houses and dine upon rice cakes and gulps of milk, and somebody would strum a guitar casually while the television echoed softly in the background. She would zone out and fall asleep, and these four boys would watch her innocent body as her chest took long and gasping breaths, cover her in a blanket, and turn off the lights. No phones ever rang to demand why she'd broken curfew, again.

She spent the winter on one of their couches, shivering and afraid of something.

The forest is full of monsters and things that go bump in the night, the things hiding underneath your bed and in your closet. As the days and weeks and months dragged on, it became clear to the four of them that she was hiding monsters underneath her skin.

One day in May the sun came out to play. She'd shed her skin and started daring to wear skimpy clothing and they all saw the damage that had been done, her body decorated in an array of colors, fading and fresh bruises. She was a mess of hues – blue eyes tinged a permanent red, always lined in black and blue, green fingers wrapped around her wrists lined in a sickening ochre, hair that she used to enjoy dying green was now stained black to match her moods, pale skinny white legs frozen red and now dappled in bruises as well. All of the colors that she had hidden so well with layers of clothing she now showed off proudly; she could trust these men.

She strode through the forest full of confidence where others would be afraid, just to prove she could hold her own and theirs, and they held her hands. They stopped for their obligatory smoke break. They hoisted her up on to two sets of shoulders and told her not to scream. They got her good and stoned so she wouldn't be afraid. They had leftover ropes dangling from their pockets.

She was paraded around as a queen throughout the woods for a good while before they finally dropped her to the ground and she fell to her already scraped knees and enjoyed being high and looking at the sun peeking out through the trees still covered in snowy tips. They removed the rope in case restraints were needed. They pulled her to her feet and forced her to walk with them for a few more yards and again, made her promise not to scream as she held her hands over her eyes.

In a slight clearing, void from snow, green grass was peeking through and they led her through the opening, two in front and two behind, boxing her in the middle. They told her to open her eyes.

There was a monster tied to a tree, a monster in the disguise of a grown man she had once grown to trust. His mouth was covered, but she could hear his grunts and she plugged her ears and vomited at the sight of him. They handed her a stick, a leftover one that they had once used as a shovel, and she gripped it firmly in her hands as she faced this monster.

She painted him as he had her. She hit him and heard a crack; it could have been the stick or his nose, but blood poured freely and the sun shone on her face as tears flowed and she beat him mercilessly. The monster grunted and cried, and when she was done, she dropped the stick and ran back to the comfort of the four of them. They sparked a joint and let her inhale what she needed to feel okay.

One of them picked up the stick and had his way with him. Bones were shattered as this monster stood helplessly tied to a tree, accepting his defeat.

One by one, they each took their turns decorating this monster's body in the same color bruises he had been inflicting on her for months now, possibly even longer than they had known her. As the sun started to set, his bruises were becoming more visible, even in the dark. He hung his head in defeat and begged for his life with his eyes.

The four boys untied him from the tree. He was too weak to fight back and the extra ropes, no longer necessary, still hung from their pockets. They lifted him above their shoulders, as they had previously lifted her, and carried him. They carried him throughout the woods to a very special place that the five of them used to haunt faithfully.

Their hole that had grown to dynamic proportions was no longer filled with snow and ice, but instead a thin layer of mud splattered upon the five of their faces and mixed with the blood of a monster as they threw him inside of it. One of the boys handed her a shovel, but she shook her head and picked up a pile of earth with her hands and threw it inside. Each of them followed suit and the monster lay inside his grave with wide eyes and broken bones.

She paused and the four stopped throwing dirt and rocks as well.

The silence stretched on forever before she finally broke it.

"Burn in hell," she declared before scooping a large pile of dirt upon his face. He could no longer breathe and no longer torment her. Within the hour, the grave was filled and the sun had set. The five of them stood no longer around, but now upon, the grave of a monster and smoked a joint while he suffocated underneath, buried alive. She smoked her first and only cigarette right there as he died underneath her.

They knew their way out of the forest without flashlights. They lifted her upon their shoulders and paraded her out of the darkness and into the glow of streetlights, the five of them covered in blood, dirt, sweat, and tears. They knew now that all of their demons had been laid to rest.

Four boys and one girl had entered the forest the fall before, and that spring emerged four men and one grown woman. She could hold her own, and theirs as well. She was still decorated in the colors of her tormentor's abuse, but these would fade in time. Slowly, the meat would begin to grow back upon her emaciated body and she would start to grow into a woman's body to match the heart and head that she had donned since her torture had begun. She would grow up.

They would make sure of it. Their little mascot, their little sister, their paramour, their love. They would help her grow and form into the person that she could be.

Within a few weeks, the five of them ventured out to the woods and stood upon the grave, none of the dirt disturbed, and no trace of a decomposed stench.

In only six weeks, her bruises had nearly faded away completely. Her arms held more muscle and her legs more girth; a once-sunken stomach was now slightly rounded. Her eyes that were once lined in black were free of all traces of makeup, and her slightly tanned face shone bright in the sun as her eyes sparkled, staring fascinated at the wonder of the rebirth of the earth around her. Birds sang in the trees and spiders spun their webs.

One of them pulled out a joint, lit it, and passed it around. When it reached her, she instinctively grabbed it to take a nice long toke, but instead looked at the wonder of the world around her. She passed it on.

As she stood upon the demons that had once possessed her soul, she realized she no longer had anything to escape from or to. The past was the past and could no longer haunt her. She never needed to come back to this place again.

The four of them understood, tossed the joint, and ground out the rest of it with their feet.

This time, she led the way out of the darkness and to the street; they were content to follow her anywhere and never dream of stealing her crown. When they got to the asphalt, she turned around with a big white grin, the first time they had ever seen her genuinely happy.

The five of them shared a secret, and a linked connection that would follow them to their own graves. They were bound by the things that they knew and had done, and the four of them would do anything to protect her and keep her safe, their mascot, their paramour, their best friend, their little sister.

They would make sure the sun was always shining in her world from here on out.

Shade of Blue

Dalian Graylocke

Why does it feel like
Every time I get close
I feel like I'm drowning
I feel like I won't find peace
I feel everything that you told me
That I'm worthless
That I'll never be anything I dream
But I know better now
I know better now

You face me
And I'm like a lost enemy
I turn away
Before you can hurt me again
And I faced this before
And I know what it's like
And I talk to you
Like I'm just a child
And I brace myself
'Cause I don't know anything else
Take me away from here
'Cause I don't belong
But I will learn to be strong

Maybe someday I'll paint the sky blue
Maybe someday my heart will be rid of you
And I won't feel so haunted by the things you do
Twisted inside
And I'm lost in the dark skies

The meadow
The night coming on
And you were just too strong
Just like anyone, I bleed
And this time I will scream
And you won't be able to take it back
The roses are all blue and black
And nothing was left intact
And I'm blaming you
But I don't want to...
I don't want to!

Maybe someday I'll paint the sky blue
Maybe someday I'll be rid of you
And I won't feel so haunted by the things you do
Twisted inside
And I'm lost in the dark skies

And I feel like I won't know peace
'Til I say what I need to say
Maybe someday I'll know what love looks like
But I'll never find it this way

And I'll paint the sky my own shade of blue…
And I'll paint this sky my own shade of blue....

To hear the full song by Tomi Kaiser, please visit:
http://bit.ly/1vUUo9s

Sleepwalker

April Salzano

The little boy would sleepwalk
the halls, bundled in footed pajamas.
With eyes wide open,
not seeing, he made each night a journey.
Down the stairs, into the bedroom
to sniff his mother as she slept
lightly, awaiting his arrival.

She carried the child's weight back
up the stairs, sneaking, a criminal in her own home.
Mother touched daughter, who woke without words,
right on cue. They nodded through the thick dark
and made the exchange. He would sleep here
until the girl carried him back to his own bed.
Careful, before the father's eyes opened,
already angry.

During the crucial hours,
the girl would not sleep, every muscle ready
to rush her brother down the hall
or to cover his mouth and rock him
when he sobbed in sleep. She owed this
to her mother, for the time she was told
to go get the police and stood frozen by the door.
She owed it to her brother, the baby,
who had already worn a handprint on his cheek.

In the morning, he would unfold
in his own bed, never knowing
he had left.

Coming Down

Jessica Drummond

He spends his weekends
with needles and pills,
sodomizing his little friends.

Pushing the plunger,
he fills his whores with hope
and other powerful drugs.

Monday morning,
he dons a suit and tie
and kisses his kids goodbye.

A Different Tune
Jill Eisnaugle

On Valentine's Day 2007, I attended a corporate radio event at a baseball stadium as a volunteer for the station's morning show. There I met the weekend disc jockey; we introduced ourselves, had a brief chat, and went about our business at the event. It was brutally cold that morning, and by the time the outdoor event had ended, everyone was frozen. I went back to the radio station building with the morning show staffers after the event had ended.

Little did I know then that the weekend disc jockey was already researching how to contact me.

By the time I'd left the building, gone to lunch, gone home, and checked my email, I found a message from the weekend jock. In it he spoke of how he thought 40-year-olds were hot (I was 26 then), how he left his first wife for the second (again, I had just met this man for the first time), and how he was attracted to me. The whole scene was weird, but I thought maybe the cold had frozen my common sense. I ignored my gut instinct regarding the weirdness and replied. When this man learned I was two months older than his daughter (he was then 52), he admitted feeling "ashamed" of his feelings for me. I just assumed from there forward he would be another radio associate I knew in my role as a volunteer.

Throughout 2007, he and I communicated via email every few months; everything seemed cool and kosher. His mother passed away in November of that year and I called the funeral home to offer my condolences – which, to me, was the right thing to do. About a month before his mother's passing, he'd told me about meeting a woman through a personal ad and how she did not want him to care for his mother, how she was a mean-spirited woman, unlike me – a sweetheart. He made the first reference to him and me in a relationship; I laughed and blew it off.

∞

I saw the man for the second and last time in my life on Valentine's Day 2008. Again, we spoke briefly. A week after that, I left my volunteer position at the radio station. Despite this, the DJ and I remained in contact, speaking every few months, with no major concerns. There were loose references made by him in which he discussed how I'd be a great fit in a porn film or how I'd look good in black lace, but I blew this off as a joke and never let it faze me. One day, he mentioned us and a May-to-December romance (which he said would be July to December because he ages slowly) and I laughed, blowing it off with an "uh, no" response.

In 2009, the man was arrested for possession of marijuana on school property (he worked for the school system, besides the radio job). I did not believe the charges and supported him, only to later hear him say, "A little weed every now and then hurts no one." Then, I doubted him.

In 2010, the man – still involved and living with the woman he met three years before – invited me to his lake house for a weekend. My radar for odd again screamed as such and I declined the request. I did not hear from him for five months. When I did, it was the same thing: references to how I'd look good in "movies" and how he thinks I'm hot.

Just after Christmas one year, the man emailed to say that his girlfriend and he were fighting a lot and that she was an iceberg in the bedroom, making his life miserable. I read his email and said I was sorry he was hurting, but he had the right – since he owned his house – to kick her out. The next thing I knew, he said, "I would feel better and would even have a little fun going lingerie shopping for you." I ignored the suggestion.

On New Year's morning at midnight, he texted me with a "Happy New Year, sweetheart." I was the first person he thought of to begin the year. Later New Year's morning, the man – from work – emailed me approximately 40 links to ads for lingerie, dildos, and vibrators to ascertain what I liked. I began deleting these unread after I realized what he was doing and I never replied.

A few days passed and he announced that he didn't have my size but planned to guess and was heading to Victoria's Secret to shop. I – to this minute – did not think he was serious.

On his birthday, January 5th, I was very busy with work and told him I did not have time to speak to him. He said, "Well, if you're working your ass off I'd like to see that ass someday."

On January 6th, a Priority Mail box addressed to me in his handwriting arrived on my doorstep. Inside, there was a teddy, three pairs of thong panties, and a vibrator with batteries. I was furious and sickened. I contacted him and said that I didn't know what I ever did to make him think that I was interested in him but I'm not and the shipment was not cool.

He said, "I'm just a friendly pervert who thinks you're hot and I'm living out a harmless fantasy in my head." The good heart in me wanted to believe him, even despite the weirdness, so I forgave him, but I was still disturbed by the box.

Over the next week, he began texting me at all hours, calling at all hours, emailing me, and if I did not reply, emailing again asking if I was angry (with no regard to my work schedule at all). In every text, email, and voicemail, I heard, "Where are my pictures? You know I want pictures of you in your gifts."

During this same time, he also mentioned a dream he had about a woman identical to me walking naked from her shower and how he had sneaked up behind her, totally turned on by it. He said he could not type what he and this "identical woman to me" had done after that due to being on a work computer. Instead, he called me to tell me about it. I, figuring what this was about, ignored the call.

He said he guessed I'd never know the dream and asked again where his pictures were. Pictures, pictures, video – I heard this probably 300 times in one week. Finally, he said, "If you give me what I want, I'll leave you alone." I cued my webcam, put on the stuff, and trusted that he would stop. All the lingerie pictures did was make him tell me how hot I am, what all he did while viewing them, and how he wanted more than that to "make it stop."

I felt so cheap, so used, and so emotionally empty, hating myself for what I did by believing him.

∞

A few days later, his boss (a then-friend of mine) emailed me about the annual event where I'd met the guy years earlier. (I now work for a different company involved in the same event.) I confessed everything to his boss, typing it up in an email.

A week later, the DJ emailed to ask for the names and contact info of all the places I'd lived and people I'd dated, because he was "curious" and "wanted to research" it.

I immediately blocked him, putting myself into counseling to deal with the pain. My counselor had me unblock him once to see how long it would take him to communicate with me, and so I could tell him I wanted no further contact with him or else I would call the authorities; it took him less than 45 minutes from when I unblocked him.

∞

A year has passed since I was coerced into posing for the pictures. The abuser's company chose the path of victim blaming, and as a result of this, I have been blacklisted, have lost friendships with people that I suddenly realized were never friends, and have begun to rebuild my future with a voice I hope to use to educate and inspire others to speak up about their situations. Abuse should not be tolerated and silence allows the guilty to skate through life thinking that torturing others in the name of power is okay. It is never okay.

Despite my journey toward healing, there are still days on which I continue to struggle with guilt, shame, self-blame, and remorse over what I was coerced into doing. I know this was not my fault. I know he is an ill individual. I know he abused me, but in some ways, the pain still remains. He stole a piece of my innocence that I will never know again. This is the part that hurts the most.

Phantom Limb

Katie Rendon Kahn

She tells me, "I don't have a leg to stand."
It's because she still feels the tingle of the amputation;
the separation from the man who was once an extension of
      herself:
her phantom limb.

She tries on prosthetics, but they rub her the wrong way.
The separation itches and prescriptions
don't fill the prickly space once occupied by familiar flesh.

She soaks her bandages in bourbon,
but her cast won't set straight.
It feels hollow,
like empty Prozac prescriptions,
bottles of booze,
and promises.

Not Innocent (The Second Time)

Chapter 10 of *Metaphor*, Book 1
Dalian Graylocke

The open mic was set in a club designed for teenagers, and it was dark with bright lights shining all over, making patterns on the floor and walls. There was a stage right by the front window, but Adam and Shane didn't have time to look around as Michal plunged straight through the crowd to a corner booth where Emi and Regina were waiting for her.

"You're late," Regina said with a bit of a smile.

"Sorry, guys... stuff happened," Michal said, sitting down. "You guys remember Adam and Shane, yes?"

"Who could miss them with the parting sea in their wake?" Regina quipped, almost laughing. After Shane and Adam seated themselves, Michal saw that it was true. People were staring and whispering about whether these two men really were the Graham brothers and if they were still single. Adam, used to the attention, chose to ignore it. Shane, however, usually the one to encourage the adoration, had his attention fixed on something else entirely.

Regina's hair was fixed up in its usual braid, but there were rebellious kinky curly wisps sticking out here and there. Without warning, he reached for one and gently pulled on it, which excited a reaction out of Regina.

"What the hell are you...?" she began, but Shane only smiled, which somehow disarmed her.

"So you really are a curly, red-headed step child." he commented jokingly.

"My hair is not red! It's brown with red undertones!" Regina cried, covering her head.

"Sure, sure, whatever you say," Shane replied, folding his hands and staring at Regina. Michal was sure she'd never seen Regina blush like that around a guy, ever.

"We signed ourselves up for third," Emi explained to Michal while Shane was flirting. "We weren't sure exactly when you'd get here."

"That's fine," Michal said, turning her attention to Adam who was gazing at her the whole time. "Do you need anything?" she asked him.

"Don't trouble yourself. I'll get some drinks."

"Soda is fine for us," Regina said, her arm raised and her finger pointing down at the table. Michal and Emi laughed, falling into each other. As Adam stood and left the booth, Shane looked like he was concentrating on something very hard.

"I bet you'd look really cute in a sleeveless top like the one Michal has on. Aren't you hot?" Shane asked her. Regina stared at him with an odd expression Michal had never seen before.

"I don't like to show off a lot of skin." she commented drily.

"Seems like a shame to waste such pretty skin," Shane said, his tone dripping with charm. Even Michal blushed at Shane's "open warfare" approach.

When Adam returned, skillfully carrying more cups than he should have, Shane leaned into Regina's shoulder to make room and she gasped in pain.

"Oh, I'm sorry..." Shane said, moving immediately. Regina rubbed her shoulder.

"It's nothing. I ran into a door handle this morning and it still hurts. Probably bruised it," she muttered.

"Are bruises something to be ashamed of, Gina?" Shane asked, his tone so low only she could hear. She stared at him, all the color draining from her face. Shane just smiled.

Adam, Michal, and Emi all busied themselves talking about the show, but Shane and Regina might as well have been in another room. Shane had cornered her and she didn't exactly like it. She'd waited so long for someone to notice, surely it wasn't....

Shane played with the straw in his cup, stretching out in the booth.

"Tell me about yourself," he said and flashed his baby blues at her. Regina felt a tingle in her spine when he did that.

"Well, what do you want to know about me?"

"Anything. Try something trivial... like, hey, I'm Shane Erik Graham, 22 years old. I have a little brother that I might be overprotective of and I worry that I'll start balding at the back of my head."

Regina laughed, her guard dropped. "Sure. Regina Charlotte Price, 19 years old, with three little brothers and one little sister that I would die for. Why didn't you mention your parents?"

Shane shrugged, tilting his head this way and that in a noncommittal gesture. "No particular reason, I suppose... you know, except for the fact that they're dead and all."

Regina bit her lip. "Sorry. I knew about that." She looked and sounded a little embarrassed.

"Now your parents... they're alive?" Shane asked, drinking from his cup while trying not to lose eye contact. Regina thought it was cute.

"My mom isn't around much. She works two jobs to support the family. She makes sure she has Saturdays off, though, so she can spend it with me and my siblings. My biological father died. He was driving a motorcycle and was hit by a truck running a red light. My mom remarried and had two boys and a girl with my stepfather."

Shane watched her carefully as a tick appeared when she spoke of her stepfather. She clutched at her chest. Shane kept his mask on, but he was putting the pieces together. "You get along with you mom?"

"I love her to death, but when she's gone I have to help out with my brothers and sister," Regina said. Her hand fell away.

"What are your siblings' names?" he asked.

"Well… my full brother is Josh, and then my other two brothers are Harry and Louis. Lastly is my sister, Clara." Regina spoke of her siblings fondly, her features softening.

"What about your stepfather? What's he like?" Shane asked.

Regina's bright expression darkened vastly. Her hand touched her chest again. Shane was very sure now. "Frank is… kind of a freeloader. He works hard in the summer at his construction job, though."

"You don't like him," Shane said, setting his drink down.

"Not especially. We have to get along, though. He's my mother's husband…." The expression Regina had on her face disturbed Shane. It was like she was trying to convince herself. He put his hand on top of hers and she suddenly snapped out of it and looked up at him.

For some unknown reason, that act of kindness brought a tear to her eye and it spilled down her cheek.

Somehow, he knows, Regina thought to herself, horrified by the idea. She wanted to yank her hand back, to scream at him that he knew nothing, but she couldn't. Something about Shane Graham had her disarmed.

"If you're 19, why don't you leave?" he asked, lacing his fingers into hers. The gentle touch brought Regina such bliss, but she'd never tell him that.

"My siblings. I can't just leave them…."

"What about college?" Shane asked, suddenly much closer to her than he'd been before.

Regina almost recoiled. She knew Shane's reputation. The last thing she needed was to fall for a playboy.

Wait, fall for him? Oh, great. "I n-never had any plans…." she stammered.

"There must be something you want to do with your life," Shane prompted. Regina couldn't think straight with his hand placed so tenderly on her face. Her heart was racing and for once it wasn't from fear.

"Police," she said suddenly, unsure where it came from. Shane gently rubbed her cheek with his thumb and smiled at her softly.

"You like being a protector," he said, his words somehow mesmerizing.

"It's all I know," Regina replied.

Suddenly she became painfully aware that everyone at the table was staring at the two of them. Shane didn't seem to care at all, which made Regina feel like she shouldn't care, either.

She didn't know who instigated it, but suddenly their lips met and she closed her eyes, enjoying the kiss. She opened her mouth a little and Shane took advantage.

Michal shot Emi a look, while Adam was left wondering what just happened.

Shane and Regina pulled away at the same time, both of them glancing at Michal for some reason. Adam knew why Shane shot the guilty look at Michal, but Regina seemed hot, bothered, and somehow at a loss. She excused herself quickly and grabbed Michal as she left the booth, dragging her to the bathroom.

"What hell just happened to me?" she asked Michal, safe in the confines of the bathroom. That man was going to ruin everything!

"That's what I was wondering. You never really seemed interested in guys before," Michal said, leaning against the sink and staring into her own eyes which looked lavender in the mirror. Was that a trick of the light?

"What do I do, Michal? I kissed him!" Regina cried, panicked.

"Enjoy it, I suppose," Michal said, putting her hand on Regina's shoulder.

"But--" Regina said, her voice sounding a little drained.

"Stop making excuses... tell me what's going on."

"I would if I knew! He makes me feel... something, I don't know!" Regina cried, grabbing Michal by her shoulders and giving her a little shake. "Tell me what you know about him!"

"Fine, fine!" Michal cried, shaking free of Regina's grasp. "He's surprisingly sweet for a guy who has probably had sex with every single girl he's ever met. Honestly, I don't think he's even on bad terms with any of them, either. It's probably because he's honest with them from the beginning." Michal deepened her voice, "Uh, ya know... I just want have sex. No strings attached, not commitments... just sex."

Regina shook her head. "How can anyone fall for that?" she asked.

"Maybe it's because most of the women Shane meets are that shallow and he doesn't try to kid himself," Michal mused.

"What do I do, Michal?! He kissed me!" Regina cried, burying her face in her hands.

"I thought you kissed him?" Michal replied, a smile in her eyes.

"Michal!" Regina whined. Michal laughed.

"Enjoy it. G, I've never seen you get excited about a guy. I mean ever. Shane's not a bad guy. Take some time to get to know him and make a decision based on that."

Regina looked down, completely apprehensive. "Could I really...?"

Michal smiled at Regina. "You can go as slow as you want," she said, trying to be encouraging.

"Okay," Regina said, checking her hair in the mirror. The bathroom door opened and Emi came in.

"Um, sorry guys. We're up," she said.

Regina tapped Michal on the shoulder and smiled. "Let's go."

∞

Shane watched as Regina left with Michal and Emi excused herself to check on the rotation. As soon as the boys were alone, Shane leaned over the table and whispered to Adam.

"I think Michal's friend Gina is in trouble at home. Could you...?"

Adam's eyes widened and he stared at Shane. "What makes you think...?" Adam began.

"That girl smells like sex and candy... seriously, whenever she talked about her stepfather, she got nervous."

"You would be able to tell the difference between a virgin and a..." Adam cleared his throat. "... fine."

Shane watched with an air of disinterest as all the girls got onto the stage, resting his jaw in hand. Adam stood and slowly moved to the stage as the sound of haunting music filled the air. Michal began to sing by the time he was within range to examine Regina.

"The rain glitters from the sky like diamonds, reflecting all that's in my heart. And you may be wondering where I'd gone off to, but I was too hurt to stay...."

Adam concentrated on Regina and almost recoiled from what he saw there. Regina's body screamed abuse in every single sense of the word. She had old breaks and lots of bruising. This abuse had to have gone on for a few years at least. Adam frowned and bit his thumbnail, and suddenly the words Michal was singing got his attention.

"As I walk the streets of brightly colored lights, I realize that I'm a shadow. There are so many people smiling happy smiles and I can't even shed a tear."

Adam looked up at Michal, suddenly realizing the subject matter she was singing about. The melody and words sent Adam back to a time that seemed so long ago when he'd been desperately trying to find her.

"And you may be wondering where you can find me, but I... I won't be there. I was touched by the cruelty of men and I move on one step at a time. And I'm tired of playing the game, I needed to be a little closer to God, I wish you'd stop comparing me to who I was... I'm not innocent. I'm not innocent. The rain glitters from the sky like diamonds and I'm not innocent. Not innocent...."

Michal was on the verge of tears when she finished the song, Emi looked pleased, but Regina seemed disturbed. Michal stepped around from the keyboard she had played for the song and jumped from the stage into Adam's arms.

"We may not have had the best of beginnings, but look how far we've come," he whispered to her, stroking her long hair.

"And where would I have been if not for you?" she whispered painfully, sobbing.

"I love you. I love *all* of you," Adam reminded her. Michal pulled back and she was smiling through the tears that streamed down her face. Adam gently brushed them away with his thumbs and kissed her gently, which garnered more attention that it ought to have since Adam was a pseudo-celebrity.

"Let's get you something to drink," Adam said, ignoring catcalls and jealous sighs. He took her hand, led her back to the booth, and sat her down. Shane watched his brother, but for the moment, Adam ignored him, his priority being Michal.

Emi and Regina came back to the table and sat down.

"Did you hear the crowd?" Emi asked, glowing with pride for her bandmates. Regina sat down looking drained.

"Michal, that was one emotionally charged song," she commented. Michal smiled at her friend and squeezed her hand. Adam wondered if Michal knew. He stood and motioned for Shane to follow and they walked over to the bar.

"Another round of soda, please," Adam said, placing a twenty on the bar. He then gave his older brother a very serious look. "Let me ask you this... why do you care?"

Shane had to consider the question for moment. "Does it really matter? I like her and she's Michal's friend. Aren't those reasons enough?"

Adam frowned. "I wanted to know if you planned on intervening," he said, looking down at his hands.

"So there is abuse," Shane said, a little winded with shock. He'd been hoping it was his imagination.

"It's worse than that, Shane. She's been beaten for a while. A few years at least, judging by the injuries. And then there's... Shane, she's been raped. Repeatedly." Adam squinted at his hands as if they were offensive.

Shane's jaw muscles flexed as he clenched his teeth. "You're sure?" he asked, looking into Adam's eyes.

"I wish I could say I wasn't," Adam returned, looking back up at his brother. "Be careful. Michal was hard to manage right after with all her insecurity... but I knew her. You don't really know—"

"I know a girl who needs someone to help her," Shane growled. Adam frowned as a tray of drinks were deposited on the bar next to him.

"But she doesn't know you. That's all I'm saying... be careful, Shane." Adam picked up the tray and left his change on the bar. Shane stayed where he was, though. He was so angry, he needed to. He exhaled once and returned to the table, slow and deliberate.

"Hey, Gina. Can I talk to you?" he asked, his expression unreadable. Regina looked at her friends, her heart thudding wildly in her chest.

"Um, sure," she said, getting up. Shane took her hand and helped her out of the booth, walking with her out the back door. As soon at the night air hit them, Shane shoved his hands deep into his pockets. He was wearing a long sleeved button-up with the sleeves rolled up to his elbows sloppily. Over that, he wore an unbuttoned vest. His shirt was untucked and fell over his designer jeans, and he stared down for a while at his Converse shoes before he said anything.

He slowly brought his gaze up to Regina's face. She was leaning back into some boxes and looked absolutely seductive. She wore a red long sleeved, frilly blouse over a black dress that flared out and stopped at the middle of her thigh. Her long legs were covered by black tights and she wore tennis shoes.

Shane swallowed as he beheld her. "You're really beautiful, you know that?" he said, approaching her and softly placing his hands on her waist, bringing his face really close to hers.

"Are you going to kiss me again?" she purred, looking seductive despite her obvious nervousness.

"May I?" he whispered, leaning in so his lips almost touched hers. She closed the distance, wrapping her arms around his surprisingly broad shoulders. Shane felt well-built and sturdy, a man a girl could really lean on.

Shane broke the kiss and gazed at her, his expression somehow sad.

"What?" she asked, butterflies swirling in her stomach. Regina had never felt like this before, and she was concerned that maybe he thought she was too young. She was only three years younger, but it wasn't so unusual.

"I want to ask you something, but you have to promise to be honest," Shane whispered to her.

"Okay," Regina agreed. If she had known what he was going to ask her, she would have run.

"Is Frank the one who's been hurting you?" he asked, holding her close by her waist. Regina felt like she'd been kicked in the stomach. Usually she would have come up with some kind of retort, but she couldn't bring herself to say anything. She just stared at him wide-eyed. After a moment, she tried to break free of him, trying not to cry.

How did he know? She'd been so good at hiding it before.

Shane pulled her into him, embracing her. "Run away with me, Baby. I'll protect you. I can take you away from—"

"I can't! Don't you see that I can't? I'm the only reason my brothers and sister can have a normal, pain-free life! If I run away, he'll hurt *them*!" She leaned into him and sobbed into his chest.

Shane responded by holding her tightly, and somehow it didn't feel restricting at all. Regina felt safe in his arms, and she suddenly felt like she could tell him anything.

"How long can you shield them from him? How long until he goes too far? Regina, I care about you. If anything happened... just run away with me," he pleaded. Regina looked up at him, her makeup still almost perfect despite her crying.

"I want to. But I—" her voice broke.

"Don't. Think about it. It doesn't have to be tonight. But Gina... think about it soon." Shane broke the embrace.

"Don't!" Regina cried suddenly as his arms left her. "I don't know why, but I feel like if you walked away right now, I'd fall to pieces!" she gasped, reaching out for him. Shane gladly embraced her again.

"I was 14 when Frank first raped me," she whispered. "He comes to my room every night when my mom is at work. He pays me every time he...." Regina looked so ashamed that Shane kissed her, and he suddenly felt like a bad person for doing it. She was like a guilty pleasure and he found himself wanting more.

Her tongue caressed his and fueled the passion rising in him. It became almost too painful to resist. His hands wandered to body parts below her waist and she didn't seem to mind. He lifted her up into his arms and she wrapped her long, sexy legs around him.

"Easy," he whispered to her.

"Am I going too fast for you to handle?" she purred, kissing him again.

"Oh, God! Not if you want me to respect myself in the morning," Shane murmured, trying to control his impulses.

"I've had sex before, Shane," Regina reminded him, kissing his neck. Shane sighed and set her down gently, moving one hand to her waist and one to her beautiful face.

"That's just it. I don't want to *have sex* with you, Gina. I want to make love to you. I want to show you how I feel. You drive me crazy, but you also make me want to protect you. I want to nurture this feeling longer. Do you understand?" he asked, kissing her forehead. Regina trembled at his touch.

"I thought I was ruined for men. I never knew I could.... You've really done it, Shane... I think I'm falling for you." Regina turned pink.

"Then don't let that man touch you again. Let me save you like a proper boyfriend—" Shane turned red when he said the b-word, and Regina's face lit up.

"Tomorrow. Give me until tomorrow," Regina said and kissed him again. "I really want to know what having sex with a man I care for would feel like," she mused aloud.

"Oh, I think you'll find out soon enough," Shane replied, concurring. She laughed softly and leaned into him.

Suddenly the doors slammed open and Michal came out with, of all people, Jeff. She looked angry and Jeff looked frantic. Regina watched Shane's conflicted expression. He still stroked her hair and held her, but he seemed unable to take his eyes off of Michal.

"Come on, M! Just give me a chance to explain!" Jeff was saying when Michal suddenly spun on her heel, making Jeff stop quickly or risk running into her.

"My name is Michal, Jeff! We're not little kids anymore if you hadn't noticed, which is my point!" Michal growled at him. She sighed and brought a hand up to her head. Regina leaned in to watch, interested in the exchange. Michal and Jeff didn't seem to notice they had an audience.

"I'm sorry, Michal. But the idea that... that he touches you and... I made a mistake. I know that nothing I do now would fix that in your eyes, but I don't want to be cut off from your life. We used to be best friends... and I'm jealous."

Michal sighed and rubbed her head, looking oddly pale in the moonlight. Shane inhaled sharply. He was in motion before Regina even knew what happened.

"Mica!" he cried, reaching her just before she fell onto the pavement. Regina was just behind him, concerned for her best friend.

"What's wrong with her, Shane?" she asked, her voice panicked.

"I'm not sure," Shane answered honestly. "Baby, go get my brother, quickly!"

"What can I do?" Jeff asked, a little frantic himself.

Shane snapped his fingers at Jeff. "You can back the fuck off and shut the fuck up!" he growled. He then cradled Michal's head in his arms. "Mica? Come on, sweetheart... open your eyes," he pleaded.

The door flew open and Adam skidded to a halt, taking Michal from Shane. Shane stood and watched helplessly as Adam touched his hand to her forehead. Her long eyelashes fluttered as they revealed her strange lavender eyes.

Adam kissed her softly, keeping his lips close to her ear. "Are you okay?"

"I don't know that I can keep going on like this," she whispered to him.

"Take it easy... you're just exhausted. I'm sure with some rest...." Adam whispered to her. Shane took a step back, feeling like his heart might collapse under the heaviness of the feelings he harbored there when a warm hand snaked its way around his arm and Regina leaned into him.

"Adam... please, take me home," Michal pleaded, resulting in a hurt hiss from Jeff.

"Of course. Regina?" Adam asked, looking at them suddenly. Regina didn't let go of Shane and he gazed at her calmly, though his expression revealed how conflicted he was feeling. He was trying too hard to hide it.

"Yes, Adam?" she asked, glancing up at Shane for a moment before returning her gaze to Adam.

"I'm taking Michal home. Can you give Shane a ride home for me?" he asked. Shane blinked.

He fought with himself for a moment. On one hand, he wanted to stay with Regina, but on the other, a stupid voice kept telling him that Michal was the priority. He was losing it. He needed to sever the feelings he had for Michal. He was just torturing himself with the love he was feeling for his little brother's girlfriend.

"Sure. I'll take him home. We were in the middle of a conversation anyway." Adam nodded, picked up Michal like a bride, and carried her back inside.

Jeff sighed and went inside, too, leaving Shane alone with Regina.

She gazed at him a long time before she said anything. "I answered your question honestly. So it only follows that you answer mine," she said. Shane sighed and nodded tersely.

"Are you in love with Michal?" she asked. Shane exhaled like he'd been holding his breath. For no reason at all, he felt like he'd been holding it and a release came to him just for the question being asked.

"Nothing I said tonight was a lie, you know," he replied, not really answering her question.

"Shane. Please," she said, frowning.

"Yeah. I am. And I feel like a fucking douche bag for it, too," he growled, folding his arms.

"... but you feel strongly for me?"

Shane blinked slowly, his eyes meeting hers. "I genuinely want to protect you—"

"You want to be my knight in shining armor?" Regina asked, taking his arms in her hands and gently coaxing them to unfold.

"Fuck, no," he replied and she gasped, a little hurt, looking up into his eyes. "I'm certainly never going to wear anything shiny. Gina, there's a lot about me you may never know about, and not everything about me is good. In many ways, I'm Adam's polar opposite. I mean look at me... I fell for my own brother's girl and was making moves on her best friend at the same time... Jesus—"

Regina kissed him. When she broke the kiss, she had a little smile on her face. "Shut the fuck up."

Shane stared at her, speechless. His mind was blank, but his expression was confused.

"I can't deny my feelings for you now, and I'm not that kind of girl, anyway. But if I were standing next to Michal and something happened to the both of us—"

Shane smiled softly, weaving his fingers into Regina's hair.

"My point being that your infatuation with my best friend seems completely innocent. Michal is easy to love. She's always had that kind of power over people. I'm okay with that, really... as long as I am always first...."

"Baby, there's no question of that," Shane said, frowning. "I may need time to get over this—"

"Shane, you're an idiot," Regina interrupted. He looked at her, his eyebrows furrowing.

"The fuck...?"

"For a guy who has reportedly slept with every woman he's ever met, did you never realize that first love is something you never get over?"

"How the fuck do you know that?" he asked, raising an eyebrow.

"You're surprisingly easy for me to read. Like I know you've been harboring a serious hard on for me since we first kissed."

"... about that. Where the fuck have you been these past few years?" he asked, pulling her toward him.

"Shane... please... be serious for a moment... I don't think I'm strong enough to seriously leave an abuser just to end up in the arms of a guy who's indifferent," Regina said, suddenly serious. She trembled, and Shane realized she was hurting. He smiled softly and pulled a ring he'd been wearing off his finger and dropped it into her hand. It looked like a class ring.

"Shane Erik Graham, born August 9th," Regina read the inscription.

"You're right about one thing. I'm new to love," Shane whispered. "But I'm more serious about you than I've ever been about anything in my whole life."

Regina held up the ring, the olive green peridot gem set in the ring glittering brightly in the street light. Shane closed her hand around it. "I want you to have it, Gina. As proof that I meant everything I said."

Regina looked up at him, a tear sliding down her cheek. She pushed the ring onto her left middle finger and it surprisingly fit. Shane kissed her.

"Bad boys aren't supposed to be so honest, Shane," she almost growled at him.

"What can I say? You make me want me to be good," he purred and pulled her into his arms. "Regina Charlotte Price... run away with me," he breathed.

"I already told you... tomorrow," Regina replied with a little laugh. Shane smiled at her, took her hand, and they went back into the club.

∞

Regina was laughing all the way to the car with Shane right on her heels, his arms enveloping her the whole way. When they got to her car, an old hatchback, she turned around and Shane kissed her passionately.

"I feel like I could really let loose with you," she murmured seductively.

"Don't tempt me," Shane breathed.

"I feel safe with you, Shane. Like I could really be happy," she clarified, throwing her arms around his neck and smiling at him. She was so beautiful.

"Don't feel like you owe me anything because I want to be with you," he said, kissing her lips softly.

"I'm used to having sex just about every night, you know...." She was joking, but the comment erased the smile from Shane's face.

"Then I'll make love to you every morning," he said, gazing at her intently for a moment before opening the car door for her and helping her in. Shane sighed heavily before he got into the passenger's side.

Regina was staring hard at the steering wheel and it was a moment before she spoke. "I don't want to go home," she said, her voice trembling. "But if I just disappeared, my mother would worry. I need to at least get some stuff together and write her a note explaining why I'm disappearing."

Shane's expression was soft and inviting, and Regina was positive that she had fallen in love with him. He had such a nice face, but it was his eyes that drew her to him most. Eyes that completely knew pain and suffering.

"So... come get me tomorrow? Early, like six in the morning? If I pack just my gym bag, he won't suspect anything."

He took her hand in his and brought it up to his lips. "Such a brave girl," he whispered. "Of course. I'll be waiting for you. But I'll need your address."

Regina reached into the back of the car and pulled out her book bag. She wrote her address down for him and he put it in his jeans immediately.

Despite all the talk, Regina still wasn't ready to go. She fidgeted with the keys in the ignition and glanced over at Shane.

"You say I'm brave, but I'm so scared.... You're asking me to walk away from the only life I've ever known, and I just don't want this moment to end." She blurted it out, suddenly crying. Shane reached over and pulled Regina into an embrace, stroking her hair and hushing her.

"It doesn't have to. You and me... Adam and Michal... one big, happy family. It will all work out, you'll see. You don't have to live in fear anymore. I would never hit you or make you feel inferior. I want to show you what real love is like," Shane said, kissing her forehead.

"Okay. Let's get you home and I'll see you soon enough," Regina said with a smile. She turned the key in the ignition and they drove off. Shane turned on the radio and sang along with the same songs she loved, although he sang badly... and loud. Regina couldn't help but wonder if that was a front just to make her smile, and if it was, it was working.

When she pulled into Shane's apartment, his jovial disposition melted and he became quiet.

"Well... we're here," Regina said with a little sigh.

"Just promise me you'll be careful," Shane said, taking her hand into his.

"I will. See you tomorrow...."

"Six o'clock," Shane replied, opening the door. He walked around in front of the headlights and knocked on her window. She laughed and opened it until he reached in, took hold of her face with one hand, and kissed her fervently.

"Love you," he muttered, stroking her cheek. She smiled.

"Me, too," she replied, trying not to cry. She drove away. Shane watched until her car pulled out of sight and turned to look at a figure he'd spotted hanging around outside the courtyard.

"And who the fuck are you?" he asked, his expression dark.

A man stepped away from the building, suddenly in view. "Agent Shen Lang. I came down here to meet with you and your brother. Care to invite me in?" Shane sighed heavily and thundered past the stranger to the apartment.

∞

Regina was still a little scared, but she felt like she was walking on a cloud. She came home practically glowing.

"Reggie, why do you look so happy?" her brother Louis asked.

"Well, my friends and I won a prize at the open mic tonight."

"That's not so unusual," Harry said, sounding bored and staring at his Gameboy.

"I'm going to my room to work on homework," Regina announced and tromped past her brothers.

"Aren't you hungry?" Clara asked, sitting at the table with a PB&J on a plate.

"Nope," Regina said, turning the corner and going up the narrow stairs to her bedroom. As soon as she was inside her room, she closed the door, turned on the lights, and went straight to her closet. She immediately dressed down, packing her current and favorite outfit into her duffel bag and throwing on her night shirt. She picked the best pieces of clothes she had and stuffed them into the bag, including some of her sexier lingerie and underwear.

She then threw a box into the bag with all of her jewelry and hair clips, followed by a heavy book she'd hollowed out to hide all of her money. She zipped it closed and sat down at her desk with a piece of paper. Addressing it to her mother, she added sentiments of apology and an explanation as to why she couldn't stay anymore.

She hadn't noticed that the door to her room had opened. She hadn't noticed that, just a few feet away, a man stood there watching her as she wrote. When she finished, her attention was captured by the book case by her desk. She wondered what books she'd like to bring with her when a hand came down painfully on her shoulder.

"What the fuck do you think you're doing?" he asked dangerously.

Regina felt all the strength leave her, the only emotion left being immense fear.

"I was just going to read a book," she lied.

Frank picked up the letter she'd written. "I see. 'I lied to you. He comes to me every night and I just can't take the abuse anymore. I don't want you to think that it's your fault...' are you going somewhere, Reggie?" he asked.

Regina felt hot and cold all at once.

"And what the fuck is this?" he asked, pulling on the ring Shane had given her.

"No... no, please!" Regina begged. He pulled harder and Regina cried out, forced to straighten her fingers or have them broken.

He examined the ring for a minute. A menacing darkness subtly settled on his face. Regina recoiled as he slapped her so hard she fell backwards into her desk, holding her face. "Who the fuck is Shane, Regina?" he screamed at her, this time punching her on the side of her face, hitting her a few times.

"Stop... stop!" Regina screamed. "Please!" she cried, her face swelling. Frank stepped back and pulled off his belt in one smooth motion, whipping her with the buckle end. Regina tried to move past him to the door, but he caught her and jerked her arm so hard that there was an odd popping sound and Regina screamed.

Frank threw her into her bed and there was another popping sensation in her arm. While her left arm dangled uselessly, it also bent in an odd angle. Regina screamed, sobbing as Frank continued to beat her with his belt buckle.

"Who the fuck is Shane, you ungrateful little bitch?" he screamed at her.

"No one!" Regina cried, throwing her good arm over her head to protect herself. Frank grabbed her by her good arm and threw her onto the bed, stomach first. He took his belt, wrapped both of her wrists together with it, and pulled, causing Regina terrible pain in her dislocated shoulder.

"That's right, bitch. You belong to me," he said, reaching under the bottom of her night shirt and pulling down her underwear.

"Stop! Please, stop!" Regina wailed. By now her siblings were all in the doorway, watching, too terrified to do anything. Too young to do anything. When she felt him shift a little to pull his pants down, she tried to move away, but he punched her in the back of the knee. She screamed as it connected, collapsing onto the bed with her good shoulder, feeling intense pain in her leg. Her arms were suddenly jerked back and he entered her, kneeling into the back of her right knee to keep her controlled.

The pain was almost unbearable, both physically and emotionally, and her siblings scattered. No one was going to save her. Every time she tried to resist, Frank punched her. His favorite spot right now was her ribcage. Then he'd hit her just because. He whipped her with the belt when he was inclined, and the sex was rough and painful. Just to ease some of the pain, Regina clenched her fists so hard, her nails drew blood. The force that her stepfather was using on her was enough to push her closer to the headboard, which doubled as a book case.

She tried to think of anything pleasant just the get her through, but the memories of her happiness seemed so distant. There was blood in her mouth and running down her face. For whatever reason, Shane's new presence in her life had set Frank off.

There was an intense pain on her forehead as she was suddenly forced into the headboard and one of her trinket boxes fell down. It was made of stone and contained a small stash of money. She stared at it, feeling like the dirtiest piece of filth. Maybe this was her punishment for thinking she could live a happy life. It suddenly dawned on her that she might not survive the night, and the fear almost paralyzed her.

"Shane," she breathed, terrified, irrationally praying that her calling for him would make him appear.

Suddenly she felt a heavy blow to the back of her head. She didn't know what had hit her, but she felt sick and disoriented.

I'm so sorry, Shane. I just wanted to be with you. Please... don't blame yourself for my death. I just got a little careless. The door... I should have locked the door....

Regina felt the world drift away. The pain lessened and then there was sweet oblivion.

∞

Shane opened the door to the apartment and let the agent in.

"And you're a replacement for...?" Shane asked, testing the new guy.

"Agent Durham. It was a shame when we lost him. He was a real advocate for ARCs."

Shane stared at Agent Lang. "The fuck is an ARC?" he asked, sitting down. He had a bad feeling suddenly, but he wasn't sure why.

"ARC... an ANGEL Registered Chosen. I think you guys are an amazing asset," Agent Lang explained. He was met with a surprised stare.

"That would be new. I thought everyone thought of us as blemishes on society." Shane stared at his hands, trying to place his unease.

"Where's your brother?" Agent Lang asked, looking around.

"Probably in his room with Michal... don't ask me what they might be doing in there, though," Shane replied, staring at his fingernails.

Agent Lang made a face and was about to say something when his radio went off loud and unexpectedly, making him wince. "Shen!"

"Yeah, Gypsy?" he asked into the radio, his voice polite.

"Is Shane there? He needs to move with you... NOW! Shane, it's Regina!" Flora's voice cried out desperately on the talkie.

Shane was out the door so fast, Shen wondered how he could move like that. Shen managed follow close enough and was surprised that Shane seemed to know exactly what his car should look like.

"You have a siren?" Shane asked, standing by the nondescript black sedan. Shen nodded.

"What's going on?" Shen asked, getting into the driver's seat. Shane was surprised to find Flora already in the car. She must have driven out with him, but had opted to stay in the car. Weird.

"A girl is being beaten to death. If we can't get there in 15 minutes, she's going to die." Flora sounded panicked.

Shen sped off, his siren blaring. It was the longest 13 minutes of Shane's life. When they got to the address, he marveled at the odd bi-level trailer. What concerned him more were the screams in the air. They chilled him to his bones.

He was off out of the car, jumping impossibly high to the second floor of the structure where the screams were coming from. He pulled back to punch through the window, his fist turning black. The shards of glass bounced off his skin, having no impact, and he jumped into the room.

Regina was now unconscious, her face bleeding and swollen, a man dropping a bloodied object and pulling out of her, fumbling to get his pants back on.

"Who the fuck are you?" the man asked nervously.

Shane's face was half sorrowful, half enraged. His gaze moved to Regina, motionless despite having been quite alive just a few hours ago. "Gina?" he called softly, his voice trembling.

A fist struck his face, turning it away from Regina's limp form. Shane turned his head back slowly, his face now twisted into an expression of demonic rage. The pain in his jaw was nothing compared to the pain in his heart. He brought his knee up hard into the man's crotch. The scream the man let out indicated a retrieval surgery might be needed in the future. If he had one.

Shane wasn't sure what happened. His vision went white and he just wailed on the man, beating him in the head repeatedly.

He was pulled off suddenly.

"You will calm yourself now, Spear!" Shen commanded.

Shane immediately crawled onto the bed. He was no paramedic, but he knew she was in trouble. Her head was bleeding, the left side of her face swollen, her eye swollen shut. There was blood on the bed, and there was obviously something wrong with her arm. He gently took off the belt binding her hands and curled up next to her, trying to assess the damage, which looked severe to his untrained eye.

"My God... my God... Regina... Gina... what did he do? Gina, baby, are you alive?" he asked, his voice cracking with emotion. He ran his hand through her hair. Then he noticed that she was clutching something despite being unconscious, even though her hand was now open a little.

It was his ring.

∞

Shane stood outside. He was smoking a cigarette that he had bummed from an officer who had arrived on the scene. Trembling, he watched as the EMTs stabilized Regina, putting her in a neck brace, setting her arm back into its socket, and putting her on a gurney.

He took a deep drag, filling his lungs with smoke before expelling it slowly into the air. Shane wasn't a smoker unless he was stressed. It forced him to breathe deeply when he really didn't want to.

Sadly, it looked like Frank Talbot was going to live, at least for now, but he was going to need reconstructive surgery and would probably be brain damaged when he woke up, if he woke up at all.

They couldn't wake Regina, so Shane figured it was a good trade to see Frank unconscious with half of his face literally bashed in. Fucker.

Shane took another long drag, filled his lungs with smoke, and held it there. He stared up at the sky, holding a bag in his free hand. Regina's duffle bag.

A woman drove up the driveway.

"What's happened?" she asked, panicked at seeing all the police and ambulances.

Shane closed his eyes. He didn't speak to the woman who was obviously Regina's mother. A police officer asked her questions about the abuse, about whether or not she knew what Frank was doing to Regina. She denied having known anything, claiming it was impossible. Frank loved Reggie.

Is that seriously what she said? "Frank loves Reggie." Shane's eyelids tightened and he tried actually counting against the anger that arose in his stomach at those words. But all it did was conjure images of Regina, motionless and bleeding on her bed. If that was what love was supposed to look like, if that was all Regina knew....

"I'll go with her to the hospi—" she began. Shane's eyes snapped open.

"No, you won't," he said coldly, every single word accented by cigarette smoke.

"Excuse me? She's my—" she began, swiveling her head toward Shane whom she hadn't noticed before. Shane pushed a piece of paper into her hands.

"Dear Mama. I've been lying to you for years. I felt so guilty, but it became sort of routine. So, I'm sorry. When you asked me if Frank and I got along, I lied to you. He comes to me every night and I just can't take the abuse anymore. I don't want you to think that it's your fault. I should have said something. When you had the twins and decided to get married a year later, nothing was going on. I was fourteen when it started. You left for work and I was taking a shower after school the first time it happened. He was the one who impregnated me. He was the reason I had a miscarriage.

"I was afraid that he'd come after Clara, so I let him enter my bedroom. He even paid me. I became his whore and I can't do it anymore. I met someone. I don't know him very well, but he makes me feel safe. I feel happy for the first time in my whole life. So I'm running away with him. Please don't try to find me. I'm in love, Mama." He quoted the letter word for word.

"Why?" her mother breathed, fighting back tears.

"You know, I don't get people like you. She had all the tell-tale signs of abuse. She covered her body. She never wore anything too flashy and she tried not to stand out. If you knew anything about her, you would have noticed. I only knew her for four days and I saw everything. The bruises on her arms and shoulders, her indifference toward boys... all of it." Shane took another long, slow drag of the cigarette.

"I assumed she would have told me—" her mother began, but Shane's anger was like a wildfire and he wouldn't let her get away with it. This older version of Regina, her own mother, should have kept her safe, should have noticed, and was as much to blame here as the man who broke her.

"It never made you wonder that Regina never really warmed up to her new father figure? That she had no plans for college or her future for that matter? I wonder if she thought she even *had* a future, and after tonight—" he couldn't bring himself to finish, trembling for what would have happened if he had been just a few seconds later.

"Oh, my God!" she sobbed. "There must be a mistake! Frank—"

Shane's glare was dangerous. "That!" he growled, his voice quiet and controlled while his anger threatened to consume him, pointing with the two fingers holding his cigarette. "Is *not* love!" He then pounded his chest with his fingertips. "I'm the man she's talking about in the letter, you know. She's very special to me. And I won't let you or your disgusting, pathetic excuse for a husband near her ever again. I wanted to let you know that a restraining order is in the works." He threw his cigarette butt at her feet. The cherry sparked as it impacted with the ground and glowed until ash covered it completely. The action made Regina's mother jump a little.

"Excuse me, are you the fiancé?" a paramedic asked Shane. He nodded and turned away from Regina's mother. "We're loading her up now."

"You can't stop me from seeing her! I don't know this man and that is my daughter!" Regina's mother cried.

"You're Raphaela Talbot?" the paramedic asked, exchanging a glance with Shane.

"Yes!" the woman cried, frustrated. She moved to join the ambulance carrying Regina, but the Paramedic stopped her, motioning at an officer. Shane hid his smile behind his hand as the police officer approached.

"Yeah, Tony?" he asked.

"This is Raphaela Talbot, mother of the victim and wife of the perp. She won't let the victim's fiancé go with her."

"Mrs. Talbot, what seems to be the issue here?"

Raphaela's voice began to shake as she spoke. "Reggie has no fiancé. She doesn't even have a boyfriend! I don't know this man and he claims to have some kind of ownership over my daughter!"

"First, ma'am, this is the young man who saved your daughter from being killed by your husband. Second, you should really worry about your other children who witnessed what you claim couldn't possibly have happened. Especially your son, Joshua. He's really tore up about it. I would suggest you worry about your other four kids and leave your daughter to the professionals for now. As it is, there is a restraining order being filed against you for negligence, so you're going to have to take it up with a judge before you can even think about seeing her. You're free to go, Mr. Graham." The officer waved Shane away.

Shane nodded and followed the paramedic to the rig, ignoring Raphaela's sobbing. As he was still in earshot, he heard one of the seven-year-old sons ask his mother, "Why did Dad do that to Regina?"

Instant Karma. Explain that as "Frank loved her" now, you pathetic bitch! Shane thought.

He then stepped onto the rig, preparing himself for what promised to be a long night.

∞

Shane was standing in the ER hallway, wishing he'd had some of the same privileges that his brother had. Regina was brought into the hospital and he was told to wait in the hall. He wasn't even in ANGEL, which made things all the more frustrating for him.

He propped himself against the wall and leaned his head into it, contemplating asking someone for another cigarette when the doors opened and Regina's doctor came out.

"Mr. Graham?" he asked, looking Shane up and down. Shane's shirt was a mess of spattered blood and he looked disheveled, his hair falling over his forehead with unruly abandon. Shane's cheek was bright red from the punch he'd taken from Frank, but it didn't bother him at all... she was all that mattered.

"Yes, that's me," Shane said, lifting his head.

"Regina is suffering from a mild to moderate concussion. The concern here is when – or if – she'll wake up. Her arm was cast and she has a sling she should wear for a couple of weeks. I was told this was domestic abuse?"

Shane didn't like the tone nor the look the doctor gave him. He flashed a half smile. "Her stepfather didn't approve of her having a boyfriend."

"I see. It would explain why she was clutching this for dear life," the doctor said, holding up Shane's class ring. She had still been holding on to that thing? If Shane didn't feel so anxious, he might have been flattered.

"Yup," he said simply, feeling another surge of anxiety. "Can I go see her?"

"She's going to be transported to the MRI in a few minutes—"

"Just for a minute. Please," Shane begged, putting on some Graham charm.

"Just for a few," the doctor said after a minute and showed Shane to Regina's room.

Shane took her hand and clasped it in both of his, pressing her cold hand to his warm forehead.

"You promised me you'd run away with me. What am I supposed to do if you die on me?" he whispered softly and freed one of his hands to stroke her hair.

Regina's eyes fluttered and she moaned softly. "It hurts...." she whined softly.

Shane got a little excited and gasped, leaning in close. "Regina, baby, can you hear me? Open your eyes...." he pleaded.

Suddenly her baby blues were trained on him and tears spilled out. "This is your fault," she said, that whiny quality still in her voice.

"I am so sorry," he breathed. "I smashed his skull in and I kicked his balls so far up his body, he will probably never be able to use it again."

Regina laughed softly at that, which turned into a sob. "Shane, he would have—"

"Shh... I would never have let that happen," he said, stroking her hair again.

"How did you...?" She began to ask him, suddenly aware that she couldn't move her neck.

"Easy! You have a neck brace on. Call it intuition... I just had a feeling something was terribly wrong. I have a friend in enforcement and he came with me. Your stepfather is going away for a long time. A long time being at least 30 years, I hope. And you'll be safe and out of his reach by then... and your siblings will be all grown up by then."

"Oh... thank God... hearing that makes the pain worth it." Regina sighed.

Shane pressed the call button. "Baby, how much pain are you in?" he asked, his fingers caught in her blood-soaked hair. He gently pulled his hand away.

"On a scale of one to ten? I don't want to sound like a baby, but I feel like I'm dying... a ten for sure."

"Nurse's station," the voice on the intercom said.

"Yeah, Gina Price is awake and in serious pain," Shane said, kissing her cheek.

"I'll inform the doctor," the intercom said and went dead.

"You owe me," Regina said, gazing up at Shane longingly.

"When you're better...." Shane left the promise hanging in the air. Regina smiled and closed her eyes, only to open them again and stare. As long as Shane was there gazing at her, she felt like she could live through anything. She used him as a focal point throughout the tests until she eventually succumbed to the drugs in her system.

∞

Michal and Adam waited for Shane and Regina to come home. Agent Lang had stopped by to explain who he was and what had happened. Ever since then, Michal sat on the couch, occasionally drifting off while Adam mindlessly watched TV.

When Shane finally came home, he had Regina in his arms, and without a word, he brought her to his room, putting her into his bed. When Regina was secure in bed, he left his room and walked out into the living room. Michal and Adam stared at him expecting answers, but all they got was Shane's sagged posture, his face crumpling. He began sobbing suddenly.

Michal looked at Adam, who looked alarmed. She walked up to a Shane and threw her arms around his neck, and Shane reacted by embracing her tightly, burying his face in her shoulder and crying his eyes out.

While Michal the maternal gave Shane a shoulder to cry on, Adam went to the kitchen and grabbed his brother a cold one.

"He almost killed her and I... maybe if hadn't given her my ring...." he sobbed into her shoulder.

"It's going to be okay, Shane. She's home with us now. Agent Lang came by and said she was to be placed into your custody until she decides what she wants to do. You saved her, Shane." Michal spoke softly into Shane's ear.

"Why is this so hard?" he sobbed, gently nuzzling Michal's neck to reposition his head on her shoulder.

"I don't know, sweetie. But you're a hero tonight. You saved my best friend's life. It's not your fault her stepfather decided to punish her over a ring. You gave her hope. Even if she had died tonight, I'm sure she would have been grateful to you—" Shane sobbed again, leaning so heavily into Michal that she could barely keep the both of them upright.

"Shane, listen to me. Regina really cares about you. You're very special to her and you saved her life... I'm so proud of you." Michal whispered soothingly and Shane's sobbing slowed. He stood gazing at her. Michal swallowed, knowing what the look meant, even if Shane didn't realize he was doing it.

"She was hurt pretty badly, Mica. She has a mild concussion, a few cracked ribs, her arm was dislocated and broken, and one of the muscles in the back of her knee tore. They performed a few tests to see how long her body had endured abuse and they told me..." his eyebrows furrowed in pain. "They told me...." He rubbed his eyes and moved silently to the couch, throwing himself down on it.

When Adam returned to the living room, Shane was sprawled out face down on the couch, apparently exhausted from crying. His breathing was slowed and he had every indication of falling asleep. Michal was watching him, her hands twisted together and her face a mask of deep concern.

Michal looked up at Adam and smiled softly. "He really cares about her...." she whispered.

"I imagine it has something to do with you," Adam concurred, setting the beer down on the coffee table. He sighed and lifted the blanket off the back of the couch to cover his brother. Shane's breathing had evened out and it was clear he was out cold.

Adam held out his hand for Michal. She took it and he led her to the bedroom.

"Did he say anything?" Adam asked pensively, removing his watch and his clothes. Michal wasn't sure she'd ever get used to Adam's naked body; she blushed, adverting her eyes a little.

"He said G had been hurt pretty bad. She has a mild to moderate concussion, some cracked ribs, a dislocated and broken arm, and then he broke down saying something about the damage to her being so severe... he couldn't finish the thought. He just laid down on the couch and fell asleep."

Adam sighed and sat next to Michal, now dressed in nothing but pajama pants.

"Are you okay?" he asked, pulling her into his arms. Michal sobbed a little into his chest and he gently caressed the back of her neck with his fingertips.

"I didn't know... if I had known...!" she cried into his collarbone.

"Michal, honey, she didn't want anyone to know. What happened tonight was just... Shane saved her for you. He saved her because he likes her. She's going to be okay now," Adam reassured her.

She lifted her head and kissed him softly, which quickly turned into a more passionate exchange. One thing led to another before they went to sleep.

∞

The peace of the night was shattered by the sounds of desperate screaming.

"Shane!"

Shane was up like a shot, and though Adam and Michal's room was closer, he was there before they were.

"Gina? Gina, baby, what's wrong?" Shane asked, terrified that maybe they had missed something, that maybe she was in pain, or worse, that she was having a flashback.

"Shane? Shane, where are you?" Regina screamed, her eyes rolling about wildly in her skull. Shane crawled under the covers, curling his body against hers and tucking one arm under her neck, curling his arms gently around her battered and broken body. Adam and Michal just watched, a little terrified.

"I'm here, baby, I'm right here," Shane murmured into her ear. Regina's expression relaxed a little.

"Hold me... please! Hold me...." Regina sobbed.

"I am, baby. I've got you in my arms, see?" Shane said, giving her a little squeeze.

Regina's expression relaxed. "Good... don't let go... please, don't let go...." she pleaded.

"No... no, shh. I'm not going anywhere," he reassured her, kissing her swollen face gently. Regina's breathing returned to normal and she fell back asleep. Shane's blue eyes found Adam's, whose expression was a combination of shock, fear, and concern.

"I'm really sorry," Shane began, but Adam shook his head.

"It's just a bit familiar. You got this, right?" Adam asked, putting his arm around Michal, to which she responded by curling into his chest.

"Yeah. Sorry."

"Shane... please stop apologizing. We're all just as worried." Michal's voice trembled.

"I got this," Shane said, sounding as exhausted as he looked. Michal nodded and they returned to their room.

This happened almost every two hours like clockwork. Regina screamed for Shane, waking him from sleep.

"Shane? Shane!"

"I'm right here, baby," he'd reassure her.

"Hold me, please," she'd plead.

"Baby, I am. I'm right here. I'm not going anywhere, I promise."

"Good... don't ever let go."

After the third time this happened, Shane stroked her hair gently, his fingers getting tangled in her curls. He kissed her neck, praying that the pain of this terrible night would fade quickly, especially if he had any say in it.

"You don't want me to let go... I promise I never will," he whispered to her, and he thought he heard her sob softly, but it only happened once and so he chalked it up to an involuntary spasm.

Except Regina had become lucid that time, and she heard his every word. She finally felt safe and at peace. When Shane's breathing evened out, she traced patterns on the back of his hand, trying not to cry.

She was sure she found love, and it was a relieving, painful, bittersweet experience.

"Thank you, Shane," she whispered, finally gathering her courage. She felt his lips pressed against the back of her neck and he gave her a little squeeze.

"You can cry, you know. I did, I won't lie." So she let herself cry for once, in the arms of a man she actually had feelings for, and somehow, though she felt so sad, she finally felt something she hadn't felt before.

She felt free.

Stepping Backward

Andrea Barton

"You can't rape the willing!"
you used to say to me in the morning,
grinning and still rank with last night's bender.

I beg
to differ
because when you stand wild-eyed
between your wife and the door,
make her step backward until
she falls on the bed,
and you fuck her with your feet on the floor,
your chest on her face
so you do not have to see the tears,
that is rape.
I was not willing.

I still hate the smell of beer on a body,
and when I moved from that house,
I swept up glass from the shattered window.
It was still there
under the rug,
in the crevices between the floorboards
behind the dresser.

Kneeling There

April Salzano

Pedaling fast on my rusty bicycle,
I let my hands release
the handlebars, winning. Both
my sisters trailed behind, blurring
when I turned. The damp wind
filled my sleeves, the scabs on my knees
had finally cracked.
I passed the tree that marked
our finish line, skidded to a stop.
My neighbor, whose father always wanted
to save my father, was there. Her red hair,
all but glowing.
          She took one look at me
and asked what happened, her face changed
from pink to white.
My sisters knew I could not lie;
they had to help. She asked them, too:
why bruised? I reached for a response,
but someone else was quicker:

          It was the funniest thing.
          We were all riding bikes
          in a straight line   one fell
          hit the other   who hit
          the other   and we fell
          like a row   of dominoes
                    I must have hit my eye
                    on the handlebar.

113

The neighbor said if we prayed, if we just prayed, maybe no one would fall anymore; if our father would kneel, hers could fix him.

Man of the House

Katie Rendon Kahn

My son may not remember the growl in his belly
or the sting of his father's palm,
but he remembers that I told him,
"You're the man of the house now, Baby."

He remembers his splintered fingers
from pulling up tack strips, and the smiley face
he painted before the second coat still grins
in just the right light. We made that house our home.

He remembers holding my hand
when I thought that I was holding his.
Then, when his footsteps outgrew mine,
I remember thinking that those were awfully big shoes
for a boy to fill.

He remembers the growl in his gut and the sting
of my betrayal when I brought another man home
and told him, "You no longer have to try
to be the man of the house, Baby."

Arrhythmia

Andrea Barton

It's like you died,
except you didn't.

You lurk in the chambers
of my heart.
I can feel you in there,
poking at the walls,
checking their strength
each day,
picking at my pericardium,
knowing it won't stretch,
only break.

You dismantle me
from the inside out
and I just feel like
holding my breath forever
to stop the wild arrhythmic beat
so the ventricles will crush you.

But I cannot.

I sleep instead
and see you in my dreams:
a spider whose legs have become
thrashing tentacles.
My soul is the fly
who knew better than to land
but did,
and in so doing strummed the web.

The more I dance on silken strands
the more entangled I become.
The dew drops drip
like tears.

It's like you died,
except it's me.

Just Words

A. J. Huffman

The emails and phone messages always start
out in proper tones of contrition. I'm sorry's,
Please forgive me's, and I need you's flood
the lines. If no immediate response is received,
the tone changes, indignation and accusation
creep in at the edges. After all, it is my fault
that you cheated. My lack of attention, my inability
to grant your every wish and whim and sick,
sadistic desire led to your infidelity. You devolve
rapidly into belligerence with each unanswered
communication. I am labeled
selfish, ungrateful, ignorant. You
go on, more vehemently: I am fat, ugly,
disgusting. I stop listening
altogether. Try to teach myself to un-hear
weeks, months, years of your voice.

Later my friends ask, "Why did you let him go,
he was so sweet and cute?" My response stuns.
"Tired of his abuse? He hit you?" I try to explain
the extent of the verbal barrages, the degradation, humiliation.
Their looks of commiserating outrage change
to perplexity, then concern. I am warned
about my use of vocabulary. "They are just words,
you shouldn't say abuse. People will think
he hurt you." He did. They look doubtful, mumble,
try to change the subject. They are just words. The response
ricochets in my brain. I want to scream at them,
I want to rip myself open and show them the scars
covering me on the inside.

One Step Over, Please

Maxine Moncrieffe

Just because I'm here doesn't mean I lack motion.
Indeed, you hear my cries, feel my pain, yet I will keep walking.
On and on the journey goes, completely deluded by the silence
of my heart.
Besides my fears, my Soul continues to let me know I am on the
right track.
Beauty is oh but skin deep, but the power of the "Unlimited
Mind" prevents the teeter-totter into the depths of the
unknown.
Knocked down, wrung out, left to die by the wayside of man's
misunderstandings, ignorance, and hate of self.
I will go on! I must go on! For time belongs to none, and many a
time, my drums refused to beat....
Yet here I am, once again, brought from glories not my own,
rising from the ashes like the proverbial phoenix, a
prayer upon my lips.
I said, "Excuse me! One step over, please, is where I want to go."
See, there is something that awaits me on the other side, of
Hell...
It's called LIFE.

Beautiful Numb

Jennifer-Crystal Johnson

My comfort zone,
Here in my head,
The walls
Securely in place
All around, above my head,
My heart.
The barriers
Will be
More and more
Difficult
To penetrate.

Blocked from
Emotionally
Being affected.

I love this
Hazy place.

This lovely feeling
Of no drama,
Not being affected,
And thus,
Not being
Hurt.

Wounded Butterfly

Jill Eisnaugle

A wounded butterfly fell to the ground on a winter afternoon. One of her brilliant wings had been clipped and she struggled to maintain her course. Moments before her tumble, she had become entangled in a little boy's net. While she had managed to break free, her injuries remained and she wondered if she would ever recover. Tired, rattled, and confused by how she had gone from traveling her normal, carefree path to such trauma and turmoil, she rested her head on a patch of burned out grass, trying to make sense of the events that had overtaken her life.

For several months, the sweet butterfly had endured and narrowly escaped the grips of the little boy and his net as he ran toward her using twists, turns, leaps, bounds, and mind games in an effort to capture his prey.

As the months, weeks, days, and hours passed, the defenseless butterfly became more and more tired of the constant threats to her well-being and – at the time – she did not realize the toll these run-ins had taken. It was only as she lay broken and battered, pondering the past and what the future held in store, that she began to understand the hardship she had suffered.

As she lay on the chilly ground with pain in her wing, the butterfly wondered what she had ever done to deserve the boy's attacks. Had she been too kind, fluttering around his head as if to say "Hello," and he had merely taken her advances incorrectly? Had she – in her travels – bothered him, leaving him angry and eager for revenge? Unable to rationalize such evil, the poor butterfly, beaten by life and circumstances, could not accept that she had done nothing wrong; in her battered and broken heart and through every fiber of her fractured wing, she knew she had to be guilty and the reason for her own plight.

For the next three weeks, the butterfly sauntered along, becoming more and more exhausted as she made her way along the ground, unable to fly and worried that she would never again be whole, thanks in part to the atrocity she had known. Soon, the color began to fade from her wings, malnourishment began to set in, and the little butterfly – once so full of life – began to see her very existence as hopeless, useless, and a complete waste of space. The blame she placed upon herself for not taking the little boy's attempts at harm seriously; the guilt she took to heart, feeling that in some way she had caused her situation, and her inability to understand how such evil can exist in the world began to impact her emotional well-being to the point that the butterfly once pondered crawling into a muddy riverbed and allowing the mud and muck to smother her. Her faith depleted, her strength gone, the butterfly crawled toward the river before she collapsed. Soon thereafter, she heard a voice:

"Come here, my child; rest here with me and I will ease your sorrows."

"Who's there?" the butterfly asked. "I don't see you."

"Follow the sound and come to me," the voice explained.

"But, I'm too weak to move. You see, I've been beaten, bruised, and injured; I feel like I have no strength left. I can barely see where I'm going."

Suddenly, a rainbow appeared; it was the brightest rainbow the butterfly had ever witnessed.

"Can you see now?"

The butterfly nodded, making her way to the end of the rainbow as the voice became stronger and stronger. With each step she took, she found her once nearly-lifeless body becoming stronger and stronger, too.

At the end of the rainbow, the voice was the loudest she had heard.

"Feeling better?" the voice asked.

"Yes. What happened?" the empowered butterfly replied.

"Your strength has always been there; your beauty has, too, and you are much wiser than you ever knew."

"How do you know this?" she inquired of the wise voice.

"Because I sent you to earth to do great things. You are my Creation. Now go, spread your wings, keep your head held high, and live in my light."

"But wait… what do I do about little boys with nets and people who strive to hurt me?" she asked.

"Don't worry about them. Their faith is not as strong as yours. Your heart can burn a hole through any pain they cause this world. Now, go and be beautiful."

And the little butterfly did. With her faith restored and her wing healed, she flew across the countryside, spreading a beautiful message of hope. With each flight, she shared her story of survival, faith, peace, and resilience. High and low, far and wide, she spoke of her pain, her loss, and how she was not alone as God showed her the way to health and healing.

Many times she told herself that it did not matter if sharing her story with the masses saved the world, but if her story touched just one life, then her effort was worth it. Time passed, but one day the sweet butterfly flew past a baby bird that had been pushed from its nest.

"Come with me, child," she said. "I'll show you the way to the rainbow."

∞

Throughout 2012, I was that butterfly – broken, lost, confused, and wondering how on earth I could ever recover from the atrocities I had known at the hands of emotional abuse. Because of my faith, I found my way to the rainbow, and as a result, my strength has been restored. I have found the courage to fight for what is right, even if I discovered that what is right isn't always popular. What is right and what is just: the truth is never wrong and a clear conscience is a beautiful thing in and of itself. If I can dig deep and find a part of myself I never knew existed (courage I never knew I had), I know you can as well.

Reach down deep, remind yourself of your brilliance, and then spread your wings and fly. Your life is beautiful and you are so worth it! Don't ever let anyone convince you otherwise and don't ever let anyone steal your soul. The warmth in your heart can melt away any challenge you face, as long as you believe in yourself. At the end of the day, nothing else matters.

Bruises On My Heart

Marilyn Oakley

A love I thought so perfect
A love I thought so right
A love that rose each morning
A love that said good night

But in the of course of conversations
Ugly words grew and grew
Unaware of such animosity
I didn't have a clue

A love that died daily
Making me the wicked one
A partner who saw no wrong
In the things that he had done

The things that I had learned
It was hard to understand
Why did he throw our love away
So freely with his hand?

How dishonesty and deceit
Eventually became the rule
How blind I was, I didn't see
How I became the fool

But I refuse to be a doormat
To their selfish, unloving ways
So I'm accused of not caring
Games of guilt are what they play

So unwillingly able to accept
Responsibility for their own behavior
Disrespect was their strongest weapon
I was treated as an inferior

Perhaps when they all grow up
Remorse will be a start
But will it ever erase
The bruises on my heart?

As I Rise to Face the New Day

Maxine Moncrieffe

As I rise to face the new day,
I look at things in a different way.

I smile and I look ahead,
Glad that I didn't stay in bed.

I wondered what the day would bring,
And how I used to worry about every little thing.

Having a man was like a treat,
Thinking my life, he'd make complete.

He didn't give much, but take a lot he did,
Acting a lot like a spoiled kid.

I had to sit and I had to think,
Would I let him push me over the brink?

Because if he did, oh my, what then?
What would happen to my children?

I didn't listen, I didn't heed,
My destruction was happening, yes indeed!

The lonely nights, the strange phone calls,
Him and his bitch up against the porch wall!

The life inside me tossed and turned,
Scratched at my womb as if it were being burned.

The laughing and taunting in my head,
Made me kill my baby dead.

The pain he caused me he'll never know,
It's an ache that will never go.

He talks about the evil to him I have done,
But I've never disrespected or cheated on him with anyone!

Yes I hurt him, and he feels it's much worse,
But how he easily forgets that he hurt me first.

Can we go on? Will we last?
I don't think so, too much has passed.

He doesn't love me, this I know,
For if he did, he'd never hurt me so.

No matter how much I try and try,
He still tells me all these lies.

I used to worry and flip my lid,
And try to check up on everything he did.

He's just waiting to get on his feet,
Then he'll leave me like dead meat.

Now I don't know; what's the use
To keep putting up with the same abuse?

I just don't worry, I have a plan;
I realized I don't need a man.

They're only good for a fling,
Just to get a little thing.

After that they try to hurt us,
Girlfriend, I ask you, what's the purpose?

I know that I will go my way,
It may not be tomorrow or the next day.

Things are changing, it's getting thick,
Can't you hear the clock go tick, tick, tick?

He'll come in one of these days
And everything will be gone away.

TICK! TICK! TICK! TICK!

Butchered

Andrea Barton

On a cutting board in the kitchen,
an onion looks innocent enough.
Tipping helplessly off center,
withered roots splay inertly underneath
like umbilical cords to no one.
Its skin is like old newspapers
stuffed under the eaves of the attic
where insulation should have been.
The peel is useless now,
parched, striated with hollow veins,
falls off even before I begin the task.

I approach the onion warily,
fearing its return to life.
There will be a gory battle,
between this bulb and me;
fragments of that skin will stick
to the flesh and to the blade.
Clear, potent onion blood will seep
out of each pungent raw layer,
and even if the blade passes cleanly
through the core
(yes, it has a core),
I will flinch at the delicate woody crack
of the center splitting
irreparably in half
and cringe as the halves
roll away from each other,
teeter briefly, and stop.

It will punish me then,
make me cry for my sin.
I may even have to walk away to breathe.
Yes, I know I will
have to walk away
to breathe.

Ode to Slime

Jill Eisnaugle

Like the waves of the ocean, my days ebb and flow
Some moments are peaceful; others sink below.
In a moment of strength, I smile and I laugh;
Just one moment later, I beg for a raft.
This is now my life; my life known after you…
My heart, tossed and broken; a nightmare come true.
The lies and deception, the grief and regret…
I've done nothing wrong, but I feel them; you bet.

What we shared was no friendship, whatever you say,
For friendship defined is never this way.
A friend never strives to make you two feet tall…
No, this was no friendship; no friendship at all.
The emotional rape of my spirit runs deep,
And though you don't care, this promise I'll keep:
Your toxic existence may have caused me strife
But, no matter your effort, you'll not steal my life.

Your slimed way of life has lost its appeal;
You are such a phony and I plan to heal.
So, whene'er your waves come to spew o'er my heart
I'll rise to the surface, grateful we're apart.
I'll swim toward the shoreline and bask in the sun;
I'll pump my fists proudly, admitting I've won!
For I am much stronger than you ever knew;
I'm better, I'm hopeful, I'm loved, despite you.

I live for the future, in spite of my past;
I learn from mistakes; life lessons to last.
I maintain the friendships that you tried to steal;

Unlike our nightmare, those friendships are real.
In time, I'll move past these dark days I now know
And no more will I find myself sinking below.
That day, I'll be grateful for the pain you brought
Because you will have proven all that you are not.

You are not perfection and God's gift to all.
You are not a Savior to heal those who fall.
You are not a Saint, worthy of a shrine.
You are not, nor will you ever, be mine.
You are not a hero, better than the human race.
You are not a martyr, surrounded by grace.
While I am not, either, I accept this fact well;
I do not feel the need to make earthen Hell.

On my day of healing, I'll finally see
The pain and heartache that you brought to me.
I'll find myself wiser to the likes of you
While you've slithered back to the rock pile you knew.
I'll continue my journey of wisdom and truth
Far from your existence, dismal and uncouth.
As I stand on the shoreline, I will watch you drown
Because Karma's a bitch and one day, you'll go down!

Freedom

Maxine Moncrieffe

The understanding of my emotions toward life
leaves me in a place I swore never to revisit.
Walls, barriers, and shackles are the obstacles
lining the pathway to my heart.

A dark never-ending tunnel of lost emotions and fear
dwells in the inner conclaves of my soul.
Bumping along aimlessly, bruised and battered
from journeys of old; lying down to free myself from the
          pressure.

Then, through the barren darkness shone a light
with a familiarity, causing me to search my mind's eye.
Streaming across the hallways of my inner being,
allowing me to revel in its warmth, enveloping me in its tight
          and safe embrace.

Easing my heart, mind, body, and soul,
Holding me closely,
kissing my forehead ever so gently,
setting me free in ways I thought were never possible.

Viewing myself in this old yet new light,
finally seeing myself, as if for the first time.
Encouraged to take steps
that once invoked fear and stagnation.

Leaning on the light, surely sent from the heavens,
for only there could such a force be produced.
Bracing me, holding me, guiding me along

the very path of life I was once too petrified to travel.

Thoughts of retreating to my cocoon-like haven
flood my senses,
yet the blanketed comfort of illumination
propels me forward, slowly, filled with caution.

I draw the very breath of light and life,
which for so long seemed so elusive.
I pause… I run! To the freedom
produced by sights unseen, but presence felt.

The need for continuous struggle no longer exists,
gone are the tears of fear.
Brick by brick, link by link, obstacles fading into themselves,
        reveling in
the knowledge of who I was, to who I am, and who I was created
        to be.

I close my eyes as my very essence
intertwines with the rays of brilliance,
shining and cascading over and within me,
a feeling of complete fulfillment.

A unity of forces beyond the fathoming
of the human mind,
capturing me in a grasp of radiance.

Simply Me

Jennifer-Crystal Johnson
From *Napkin Poetry*, 2010

Once upon a time,
She was me and I was she,
But did that mean I wasn't me?
I had so many uncertainties.
Anxiety had let me be,
But sadness never felt a need…
To leave.

Some time went by for she and I,
And I and she,
And now, my friends, I guarantee
That she's not me
And I'm not she….

Now, I'm simply me.

The Long Walk Home
Tiffany Lewis

The heel was long gone, but Sabrina wasn't completely sure where she lost it. It could have been when she rounded that first corner. She was unsettled and definitely not thinking straight. Maybe the heel fell off when she tripped. She ran so fast that she missed a step. No, it must have disappeared into the sewer grate. The heel was caught there, and in haste, Sabrina pulled her foot and twisted her ankle.

Sabrina was not ideally dressed for a night run: one sleeve on her blue satin and sequin dress was ripped and hanging loosely off her shoulder, her mascara showed the trail of dried tears, her foundation was smudged in swirls on her face, only one pearl earring adorned her ears, and a three-inch heel from her blue pumps was missing. The pearl necklace she was previously wearing was left behind in pieces strewn about her living room floor. Sabrina's face was also swelling quickly; her right eye and bottom lip especially. Her left arm was bruised and a handprint started to show, large and dark purple. The only aspect of her façade that was still intact was her hair. It was difficult to ruin hair that was only two inches long.

As Sabrina ran, she didn't shiver against the cold. Although it was the dead of winter, no cold could compare to the icy moment Sabrina had just faced. She still felt the chill. As if getting ready for a dinner party wasn't hard enough, a fight ensued. Her husband continuously complained about the evening, and although Sabrina knew her husband had a short fuse, she was compelled to comment. The word "bitch" set him off. After thinking in-depth about the altercation a few days later, Sabrina knew the b-word instigated the whole fight. *Stop complaining like a bitch.* As soon as she'd said it, her husband's head snapped in her direction; his eyes were large, burning like the flames of Hades.

As quickly as it had all happened, it was all over, and as Sabrina sprinted down the street, she wasn't sure what to do. The town seemed vacant. Sabrina was away from the city lights on a quiet street in a quiet neighborhood. She imagined those people were sleeping peacefully, wrapped in the arms of their lovers. Trees dotted the sidewalk, cars were parked in their driveways, and pink lawn flamingos watched as Sabrina passed. She felt far enough away from her husband to slow down, so she began to walk. Her direction seemed aimless, but her subconscious steered her the right way. She was shaken. Years of punches to the head will do that to a person. She spent five long years with her husband, and the journey had been checkered with pain, betrayal, and heartache. Sabrina was ready to embark on a different journey.

Tonight was the first night she acted against him. Not only did she fight him, she also ran from her home in an attempt to escape. She could never go back. She had blackened his eye. He would never forget that for as long as he lived. The next time he had an opportunity, he would make her pay. Sabrina thought of what might happen to her if she returned to him, and it motivated her to keep moving. She was driven to stay far away from the place she used to call home.

A perfectly manicured lawn and a short flight of stairs leading to a cozy, furnished porch invited her into the front yard. This place always invited her, even when she refused to come. When she was too busy or too sad to smile, she was still invited. When she was mean or hurtful, she was still invited. When she was ugly from a beating, like tonight, she was still invited. Sabrina carefully removed her tattered shoes and held them close to her chest like a baby that she wanted desperately to comfort. She slowly ascended the stairs, swaying as she put one bare foot in front of the other, and rang the doorbell. As she did, she began to cry.

A woman opened the door. A look of shock grew on her face. The woman gasped, and then her expression turned to sorrow. The woman held Sabrina's face in her hands and smiled warmly. Sabrina sobbed, and her head hung weakly as she revealed her soul in each tear. The woman stretched out her arms and held Sabrina tightly, her face resting on Sabrina's hair. The warmth and security soothed Sabrina. She knew she could be happy if she just stayed with this woman. She knew she would be safe here.

With every ounce of her heart resonating through each word, the woman whispered softly into Sabrina's ear:

"Daughter, you are home now."

Her Courage

Jill Eisnaugle

No one knows how she is feeling;
She hides the pain that well.
But even when she's smiling,
Her spirit lives in Hell.
Turmoil she tried to bury,
Unbearable to face,
Has risen to the surface
And is now commonplace.
Her life once held together
Now crumbles at its core;
Each day, with fears uncertain,
Now feels like such a chore.
Her peaceful rest has faltered,
The nightmares run too deep;
Her waking hours broken
Thanks to a lack of sleep.

Some days, her mind is quiet
'til painful memories bellow.
The chaos born from hardship,
So difficult to mellow....
One minute, she seems past it,
Free from its lethal wrath.
The perils formed from trauma
Leave a changed aftermath.

Nevermore will she be blinded
To the hardships she has fought;
Deep within, she has the courage
To hear with all she's got.

Some days the memories linger,
But her hope is much too great
To allow PTSD's chokehold
To be her forever fate.

Therefore, she will keep fighting,
Embracing what is real.
She'll cry whenever warranted
And feel what she must feel.
While others may not see this
Because she hides it well,
She'll face each day much wiser
Than she will ever tell.

Furnishing Gratitude

Eric Michelson

My idyllic perception of beauty
Casts doubt upon my incoherent definition of love;
I can see this thing…

This thing of which
I cast with soul-drenching lust
Behind a shadow,

Forgetting its place,
Forgetting it even bothers
Me with existence.

Is it reusable?
Doubtful…
Doubtlessly.

Doubting the job set before us,
Teeth fallen on the barren floor,
Teaching every one of us

Useful resent.

Haunted

Helen Carl

Justin fell in love with Deb when he was 17.

She was leaning against her locker and she caught Justin staring at her, again. He passed her locker every day. And every day, he would come to a dead stop in the middle of the hallway and stare at her. He didn't look at her to check her out. He had already memorized her physical appearance. He just watched her switching her books and chatting with her friends or putting on lip gloss. The last was Justin's favorite. Deb's lips were soft and full and he would fantasize about kissing them.

"What are you lookin' at?" she asked. The guy was cute, in an unconventional way, but that didn't give him the right to study her.

"Nothin'," he always mumbled and continued down the hall.

His name was Justin Scott. He had blue eyes and dirty blonde hair. It was a crowed high school and Deb had had to ask a few people to find out what his name was. Justin was one of the smart kids. He was in all of the advanced classes and had already won a few scholarships. The day before Christmas vacation, Justin dropped the bomb.

"What are you lookin' at?" Deb asked for what seemed like the hundredth time.

"You," said Justin. His confidence caught Deb off guard.

Justin handed her a scrap of paper with a steady hand. Deb looked down at it. Justin's phone number was printed carefully in black Sharpie. Deb fell in love with Justin when she was 17.

They spent every day of their Christmas vacation at Justin's house. They talked about everything and nothing, and Justin kissed the lips that had been mesmerizing him for months.

The last day of vacation, New Year's Day, Deb and Justin decided that they were ready for more than kissing. It was late in the morning when they both climbed into Justin's bed. Justin struggled to put the condom on, but after a few tries, he thought it was on good enough. They lost their virginities together.

When they returned to school, they held hands as they walked through the halls. They had no classes together and they missed each other terribly. They were still madly in love two months later, when it was Deb's turn to drop a bomb. She had missed two periods and bought a home pregnancy test. Justin sat on the edge of her bed and waited for her to come out of the bathroom. When she finally came out, she sat on the bed next to Justin and they held hands as they stared intently at the test strip. Pregnant. They were pregnant.

"Oh, my God, we're gonna have a baby," Justin said joyfully.

He should've been worried to death about his future. But instead of fear, he felt so happy that he thought he might burst. He looked up at Deb. She was grinning from ear to ear, but she also looked scared.

"Deborah, I'll always be here. I'll always love you and I'll always love our baby. Don't worry about a thing; I'll take care of you," he said.

Once again, she felt Justin's confidence warm her to her very core.

"I want to marry you," said Justin.

"I want to marry you, too," Deb said.

Three days later, Justin put a ring on Deb's finger.

"How on earth did you get this, Jus?" Deb asked.

"I wanted this ring for you, so I pawned some stuff."

They got married a few weeks after they graduated high school. But when Deb delivered, both she and the child died. Justin was eighteen when he buried his wife and son. After the funeral, he sat at his tiny kitchen table and stared off into space.

∞

Eight years later, everyone held their breath as Lina Moore took hers through a tube. Her lung had collapsed under the strength of dozens of blows to her chest and rib cage. Before the operation was even completed, the surgeon saw another serious problem. As soon as Lina stabilized, he put her on the transplant list. After 35 hours and 12 minutes on life support, her new heart arrived at the hospital. But when she woke up, Lina had a wound that no CT scan or test would ever detect. The attack on her body had broken a place in her mind, an opening through her defenses that allowed pain and loneliness to flood her every waking moment.

Her best friend, Justin Scott, came to see her in the hospital. Not every day, but at least a few times a week. Justin was a doctor himself, a very passionate obstetrician. Lina knew that Justin's success had grown from an obsession. He had lost a wife in childbirth when he was only 18 and he had dedicated his life to caring for women's bodies. He had never lost a single patient during a birth.

Justin and Lina had met at a barbeque. Justin had snuck outside for a smoke. After all those years of medical school, he still hadn't been able to kick the habit he'd picked up after Deb's death. Lina's back was to him when he walked onto the deck. She was leaning against the railing, her head raised to the sky and a cigarette pressed to her lips.

"Those things will kill ya," she remarked smartly when she heard the click of his lighter.

"Oh, I know," he said importantly. "I'm a doctor."

"Well," she said and turned to face him, "we all love things that are bad for us."

She was lovely. Her dark brown hair framed her face with soft waves and her lips were full. When she saw the expression on his face, she let out a giggle. He smiled back. He couldn't help himself. She went back to staring at the clear sky.

Justin walked up to stand next to her. Just one look. That's all it had taken. It was nothing she'd said; there was no gesture that instantly endeared her to him. He just knew in his bones that he loved her, the same way he had known that he loved Deb the first time he saw her.

He snuck a look at Lina's left hand. Wedding ring. Damn. Figures. He inhaled deeply. He hadn't felt anything like this since Deb. He couldn't be with Deb, and now he couldn't be with Lina. They had the same friends, so Justin was able to arrange it so that they saw each other pretty often. Her husband, Joe, seemed nice enough and she seemed happy. No one had known what was really going on. No one knew about her husband's temper and how he beat her.

As the weeks went by, the constant flow of visitors finally slowed and they were alone together in the hospital room more often. The nurses of course speculated that Justin was madly in love with Lina and was building up to make a move on her. But after what had happened to her, Justin doubted that Lina would want to be with anyone for a very long time.

They watched TV and played on her new laptop. Lina loved him, too; she always had. But now... now she believed that she was damaged goods. Her body was crisscrossed with scars. And it wasn't just the fact that she was disfigured and high maintenance. She was angry and afraid all the time. The brutal attack had left her heart painfully empty. She couldn't be with Justin, even if he did want her. It would only end horribly and she knew she wouldn't be able to survive it.

She almost gave in to temptation once; she almost told him. She had been walking the halls of the hospital most of the day. Her legs ached, but she was reluctant to sit down again. She still had a few more steps in her. But tears ran down her face. It was bad today. All she could see was the look on Joe's face, the hate he felt for her. Had he ever loved her?

She paced the length of her room, back and forth. She looked up suddenly to see Justin. He was sitting on her bed waiting patiently for her to notice him.

"Tell me what you need," he said lovingly.

"I don't know," she sobbed.

Instead of coaxing her to answer, he waited for her to put it into words.

"I need to know that I mattered to the man I cared about."

She sat down next to him and rubbed her face with her hands. She was still sobbing.

"Men are careless with women's hearts," Justin said, "we treat them like they don't matter and we replace them without a second thought. It's not because we don't understand, it's because we believe that you need us more than we need you."

"I already know all this," she said glumly.

"I just want you to know that not all of us are hopeless. I know it's hard for you to trust people and that it's even harder for you to trust me because I'm a man, and I'm not going to ask you to. People break their promises, even when they really mean them. All I'm asking is a chance to prove myself to you, and I'll never stop proving myself to you. I need you. I need you every day. I know you need my strength, but I need yours, too."

She let out a long, sour breath and collapsed across his lap. It was the first time she had touched anyone in a long time. He hesitated, started to go for it, and then hesitated again. Finally, he put a warm hand on her shoulder.

"I want what he promised me. I wanted to be with him for the rest of my life. He promised to be true to me, to always love me. He took all that away. I want it back," she sobbed.

Justin struggled to find the right words as Lina quickly fell asleep.

Even with her health insurance, the medical bills were through the roof. Lina would have been paying on them for the rest of her life and not even made a dent in the balance. But miracles do happen. They don't happen every day, no way. But they do happen. Lina's grandfather had passed away two weeks before she was attacked.

Her grandfather had been a fairly wealthy man and a damn good investor. She had planned to purchase only the main necessities with her money: a car, a house, an education, and then live off the rest for as long as she could. But now the necessities were her medical bills. As soon as she was off the morphine drip, she hired an accountant, hoping to minimize the damage, but most of the money still went to the hospital.

So after Lina got out of the hospital she moved in with Justin, as friends and roommates, not a couple. A year had passed and Lina was still in physical therapy but mostly back to her normal self. She had started the task of covering her scars with tattoos. The larger scars would need to wait a little longer, but her pale skin was already illustrated with delicate flowers, butterflies, fairies, and mermaids. The tattoos seemed to wrap her in a feminine softness and her self-consciousness was fading fast.

One summer morning, Lina pulled a t-shirt on over her head and checked her profile in the mirror. *Not bad*, she thought to herself. She was finally starting to like what she saw in the mirror again. She walked out of the bedroom and through the living room. Justin was hunched over on the couch playing video games. She waved at him before she opened the front door. Her new/used car was parked along the curb out front. Money was still tight, but she hoped to start digging herself out of the financial hole she was in. Two weeks ago, she had proudly handed Justin a month's rent and her share of the utilities in cash. He had been a saint to let her stay there rent free, but paying her own way gave her something she'd never had: dignity. After she paid her rent, she starting decorating her room. She moved her furniture, dishes, and linens from storage into her new place. A week later, she overheard Justin talking to one of his friends.

"Finally, a woman in your house," his friend jabbed at him.

"I hope she never leaves," said Justin. "She cooks and bakes like crazy. Her lotions and shampoos make the whole house smell good, and she's got these soft, fluffy towels in the bathroom. She lets me use them!"

Lina smiled at the memory as she crossed the front yard to her car. She tossed her gym bag in the passenger seat, got into her car, and headed for the health club. For the next hour, she glided back and forth in the Olympic sized pool. Her heart beat in her chest, her lungs expanded and contracted. Her body was finally healthy and powerful. She pulled herself up over the tiled edge. The hour had gone by effortlessly. *Tomorrow I'll do an hour and a half,* she decided.

As she showered in the women's locker room, naked and uninhibited, her mind wandered. As her body healed, her carnal cravings had also returned. In her fantasy, she saw herself standing naked in front of her locker, her scars gone. The air all around her was steamy and warm. She could hear the careful footsteps of a man walking up behind her and then pressing himself into her naked backside. She couldn't see his face, only his large hands as he reached around and explored her perfect flesh. The anonymity excited her. He knew nothing about her, and nothing was expected of her, only pleasure. She was snapped back to reality by the echoing sound of chatter. Two other women were approaching the shower stalls. Lina shut off the water, grabbed her towel, and dressed quickly.

She still loved Justin, but she had long ago put the notion of being with him to rest. She wanted an equal, a partner. She wanted to be with someone that didn't know how traumatized she had been, who hadn't seen her lying weak and helpless in a hospital bed for two months. Someone who could never guess how fucked up she really was and someone who would never view her as a patient. Then Justin asked her to go to a masquerade ball as friends. He had a great idea for costumes.

He wanted to go to the ball as a vampire couple, dressed up and covered in blood and gore from feeding. They were able to find a dark purple evening gown for Lina and a black suit for Justin. A friend of theirs, Brian, worked in a theater costume and makeup shop. He showed them a few tricks and they left with a shopping bag filled with fake blood, beautiful feathered masks, and two sets of fangs.

Brian had shown them how to mix the fake blood so that it would dry and be more manageable. They decided to get ready together, and Justin arrived at Lina's house the afternoon before the party. She was already in her evening gown, and when he went into the bathroom to change into his suit, he saw that she had laid clear plastic tarps on the floor, toilet, and sink. He chuckled to himself. The room looked like they were up to something a lot more sinister than putting on makeup.

He let Lina in when he was finished dressing, and for the next 10 minutes, they dowsed each other with squirt bottles filled with fake blood. They were having so much fun that they didn't notice the blood pooling on the tarps. In her bare feet, Lina slipped in one of the puddles. Justin was standing next to her and tried to catch her, but only ended up on the floor with her. They laughed and used the edge of the sink to pull themselves to their feet.

They faced each other, both catching their breath from laughing so hard. Before he even realized what he was doing, Justin hugged Lina close to him and kissed her deeply. His fingertips brushed her jaw line and ear, smearing the fake blood. She pulled away slowly, hating every second of it, wanting to move closer to him instead. Their lips parted, and his arms fell away from her sides. She was on the verge of tears. The idea of being with Justin just felt so big and so impossible. There were too many things standing in her way; there was too much about him that she struggled to accept. Getting so close to him was sweet and heavenly, but at the same time it stung. She could never let this happen again.

"You said we were going as friends," Lina said evenly.

"Sorry…. Do you want me to go?" Justin asked. He was devastated… and embarrassed.

"No," she said, and his face lit up.

But when she hurried from the bathroom, his hopes faded. Joe had ruined everything. He had to be the reason she didn't want to be with him. What else could there be? Then it occurred to him that they had never really talked about Joe or what had happened. He assumed she was haunted with painful memories. He knew she had nightmares and that sometimes she slept in her closet.

He had spent the night on her couch once after a same day surgery. He had woken to the sound of her screams. He ran into her room only to find her bed empty. He switched on the light and looked around the room frantically. Then he saw the light on in her closet. When he opened it, he found her curled up on the floor clutching her knees to her chest. He noticed that she was wearing one of his t-shirts. He wondered how she had gotten it; it was his favorite and had been missing for a while.

He sat down next to her and slowly pulled her into his lap. He stoked her hair until she fell asleep. He moved her back into her bed and went back to the couch, keeping the bedroom door open a crack so that he could listen to her sleep. They didn't talk about it the next day. He didn't ask how she had gotten his shirt and she never returned it. Justin knew that Lina was hurting, but he didn't fully understand why. He assumed that he did. They were close and he loved her very much. But he didn't know how she felt about herself and that she believed that she had no choice but to be alone.

She couldn't have children, her body could never completely heal from the attack, and there would always be aches and pains and scars. There would always be prescriptions and doctor's appointments. On top of that, she had enough baggage to fill three airports.

She returned with the rest of the pieces to her costume. She tried to be casual, but her hands were trembling. She hoped he didn't notice. Justin wanted to leave very badly, but he didn't know if that was the right thing to do. She was still getting ready, so she still wanted to go to the ball. But he was mortified that he had kissed her and that he had misread her signals. He decided to suck it up and follow her lead. Within a few minutes, they were both acting like nothing had happened, and by the time they got to the party, they had almost succeeded in convincing themselves it was true.

But as the night went on, their eyes kept meeting through their masks. They left the party and didn't speak the entire car ride home. When they pulled into her driveway, Justin made no move to get out of the car and walk her to her door. Lina sat and stared straight ahead with her seatbelt still on.

"I'm sorry I pulled away," she said with sincerity. "I hate that I did."

"Why did you?" he asked, his voice tainted with frustration. It had been a long night.

"Scared."

"Of what?"

"I don't know, and that makes it even worse."

He got out of the car and opened her door for her. But he did not try to take her hand as they crossed her front lawn. As they stood on the step, Lina pulled her mask off slowly and faced him. He moved closer to her, watching her carefully for a reaction. He didn't want to be shot down again. She closed her eyes. It was the sign he had been waiting for. He kissed her again, this time much more passionately.

"I'll call you tomorrow," he whispered and kissed her lips lightly.

"Ok," she said, already terrified that he wouldn't.

Justin couldn't sleep. He was still high on their kiss. He could only make himself wait a few hours before he texted her. Lina was still awake and she called him back.

"Will you go out on a date with me?" she asked as soon as he said hello.

"Yes. When?"

"Any time," she said smoothly.

"I'm off on Wednesday, so Tuesday night?"

"Ok."

Tuesday was tomorrow.

He took her to his favorite restaurant, a family-owned Italian place with a bakery in the front.

"Should I drive you home now?" he asked her. The restaurant was closing. They had talked for hours.

"No," she said shyly.

∞

They lay next to each other in Justin's bed. They held each other tight, naked and still slick with sweat from making love.

"For so long, I've felt as if I'm slowly being poisoned inside, like everything that I am is dying little by little."

"So the poison is gone then?"

"No."

"Where is the poison coming from? Still him?"

"I don't know."

Justin had hoped that making love to her would help her heal. He wanted to give her something to replace that lingering pain of being forced. He was disappointed, but he would never stop trying. But the lightness in her mood cheered him up. *Thank God*, he thought and went to sleep.

Lina spent the next day and night at Justin's. They spent the night after that in Lina's bed, a four poster hung with sheer white curtains.

She started to cry. He held her in his strong arms until her sobs quieted. He took her face in his hands and gently wiped her tears away with the soft pads of his fingers. They had a langue all their own now. Their minds, bodies, and hearts were so entwined that they no longer needed words.

"So what was it?" he asked her later that night. They were in the bath tub and she was curled against him. The warm water and soft bubbles caressed their skin.

"What was what?"

Lina cackled. It was not the answer that Justin had expected and he loosened his embrace.

"Justin, every little girl meets a boogeyman at some point. No matter how sheltered, how closely guarded, they always find us. Maybe not all of us when we're little girls, but they find us eventually. It happens to all of us."

"Was Joe your boogeyman, or had you already met yours?"

"Of course he was my boogeyman. Why would you even ask?"

"I was just thinking, I mean Joe was a bad guy, no doubt about that. But what about that guy that tried to rape you in high school?"

"What the fuck about him? I got away. When I got home I could still feel his hands on my body, I could smell him on my clothes. I took a kitchen knife from the block and I dug the tip into my arms until I couldn't feel his hands on me anymore. Then I took a hot shower."

15 years later, the scars from that day were still there, only now they hid under tattoos. Lina lit a cigarette.

"It was so weird, too. He held me so tight, but his voice was like honey, 'Don't worry, baby, I'm here. Everything's gonna be alright.'" Lina paused and took a drag of her cigarette. "I mean, who did he think he was fooling? Not me! Did he really think I was going to go for that?! What a fuckin' loser!"

Lina was getting louder. Justin was getting an uneasy feeling. She turned to him sharply.

"When he was touching me, I'd never felt so afraid. I felt like… garbage. But when I got home, I was still a virgin. He was so sure he had me, too. Soooo sure. But he didn't. He couldn't even handle a girl half his size! Pathetic!"

Justin wasn't sure what to do. Lina was lying to herself. She was so determined that this piece of sub-human shit hadn't been capable of hurting her. But she was hurting, bad. He could see that and he knew that he would never understand.

Weeks later, Lina had moved back into Justin's house. She had put almost all of her furniture into storage and thrown away the pieces that she had once shared with Joe. It was over. He was in jail, and the last remnants of their life together were rotting in a landfill somewhere.

As close as they were, Justin couldn't bring himself to find out the details about Joe's attack. He knew that Joe had raped Lina. She'd had to have reconstructive surgery on her vagina and her rectum. Joe must have been so brutal, cruel. Without wanting to, Justin would picture Lina pinned to the floor of her cheap apartment underneath Joe, crying and bleeding. The mental image nearly brought him to tears every time.

The next morning, Justin woke to Lina's mischievous smile. Justin stroked Lina's forehead. Then he rolled out of bed and walked to his dresser. He took a fresh pair of boxer shorts from the drawer and picked up a pair of jeans off the floor. Lina was still in bed, but she was sitting up. She smiled at him as she watched him dress.

"Get back here," she said with a giggle and patted the mattress next to her.

Justin flashed a mischievous smile and dove back into the bed with a running start. All she could think about was Justin's soft lips on hers, how she could feel every muscle in his body as he held her, his breath as he pressed his manhood against her through his jeans. He craved her just as badly as she craved him, she could hear it in his moans.

Their love making lasted only about ten minutes and they both finished at the same time, just like every time. Justin rolled over and lay on his back.

An hour later, Justin left for work. On his lunch break, he made a reservation at a five star restaurant and booked a luxury suite. He called a florist and ordered three dozen long stem red roses. He picked them up on his way to the jewelry store. When he walked through the shop door, his eyes went right to it: the ring he had been longing to give to Lina since the day he met her.

After the barbecue that day, he had gone to that same jewelry store to buy a birthday gift for his nurse. That's when he saw the ring. It was square cut, surrounded by a border of little diamonds that shone just as brightly. The band was platinum. It was hardly one of a kind, but when he gazed at it, he saw Lina's bright eyes staring back at him. She was married, but every time, every time Justin needed a gift, he went back to that shop and stared longingly at the ring.

"I dreamt about us last night," said Lina later that night in the suite.

Justin smiled and waited for her to continue.

"We were sitting on this gray futon style couch. I was in a beautiful blue dress and ballet slippers to match. I was holding a bowl of popcorn and I was leaning on your shoulder. You were in an all-black tux. So sleek and sexy," she said and added a wink.

"You held a remote and there was a small TV in front of us. An ocean stretched out all around us, large waves crashing into each other. What do you think it means?"

"It means we're in this together," he said confidently. It was time. He got down on one knee.

"Lina Elizabeth Moore, will you marry me?"

"Yes. Yes!" she shouted with tears in her eyes.

She knocked him to the floor with her embrace. He rolled her onto her back and pushed her dress above her waist. He made love to her passionately on the soft plush carpet.

"Don't worry baby, we're in this together. We'll never face our demons alone again. I've got you," he whispered reassuringly. "I'll never let go."

"And I promise I've got you. In my heart you are already my husband. I'll stand by you forever."

"I have an idea," said Justin with a mischievous smile. "There's a tattoo parlor about a block from here."

"What did you have in mind?" Lina asked eagerly.

Justin gazed at Lina as the tattoo artist copied her careful cursive onto his skin. She had written "I've Got You" on a small scrap of paper. It was a tattoo to be placed on Justin's chest, right over his heart. The tattoo artist had already etched the exact same sentiment onto her left breast, only in Justin's hand writing.

She had been worth every second of the wait, but he would've given anything to spare her the suffering. But she was strong, she always had been. She was slowly healing, and he would be there for her. For the rest of their lives, Lina would be haunted by Joe's brutal attack. But they would heal together, and they would fight together, no matter what.

Second Thoughts

April Salzano

The father moved from room to room naked,
loose skin hanging from his body
like torn clothing. He allowed himself
to feel free, not having to hide from his children,
gone with their mother to a funeral
two hours away. Alone
like he hadn't been in years.
He turned on the stereo and let the familiar voice
take him back to the road.
Sitting on a chair, velour against bare skin,
he rested his feet on the coffee table
and clutched the handlebars of his dismantled
motorcycle. He rode for hours
past the sun
to places he had never been:
he was a recluse
living on corn from a stranger's field,
sleeping on a garbage bag, his head under
the bike. He couldn't decide if he was somewhere
in Arizona or California,
but it didn't matter. It was the grey hour
and he was the only one on the dusty road,
alone with the crickets and the smell of exhaust.
Here he rejected that scholarship
years ago by choice.
He rode all day with his eyes closed,
and by the time he got back home,
he had forgotten just who he was.

The driveway crunched under tires.

Before he had time to hold on to the moment,
he returned like a child
to his clothing and his life, put back on
the uncomfortable responsibilities, parked the motorcycle
somewhere between the desert and the coffee table.
His wife's eyes caught his without blinking
and the children returned to what was theirs.
She saw the handlebars before she heard the music.
He looked at the fading yellow bruise on her cheek
and the suitcases in her hands,
then at the plastic gallon jugs lined against the wall.
His parents brought them
because he hadn't paid the water bill again.
He spoke without thinking:
"You can go now."

By evening, his wife and children were gone
and he knew they would be able to
survive without him.

Cleaning Up

Maxine Moncrieffe

See, I had some cleaning up to do today;
I had a whole bunch of clutter
Busy getting in my way.
As I took to the task, with no one to ask,
I stepped into the maze of my life...
I did some cleaning up today.

I opened sealed boxes, re-sealed what was good,
Lifted & inspected everything under the hood.
No more burdens, stresses, and strains.
No more out running and pressuring my brain.

Unlike or like some, I came from a poor, lost, ill-fated sect,
Born was I with feet on my neck.
Used & abused, silenced in so many ways,
Gone was my innocence, never a game to be played.
Taught no value of my body, soul, and head,
A child, oh so young, yet I was the living dead.

I no longer look at the loss,
The sacrifices, the cost.
Instead now I laugh and find joy in things,
Oh so appreciative of God giving me His blessings.
Cause, see, I had some cleaning up to do today.
I had to go through the labyrinth of my life to find my way.
Life will have tears, pain, disappointments ahead,
But trusting in God brings joy; it's what He said.

I got down & dirty, stepped deep in the grease,
But I rose up & out with God; He gave me peace.

So, I did some cleaning up today, I found a way to be set free.
I did some cleaning up today, the end product was Me.

Pain
Anonymous

Pain is something everyone goes through…
If you need help, I'll be there to guide you.

I may only be 15 years old, but at least I know
How to forget my pain and help others as I go.

I can't choose what you do with your pain; you decide,
But whether it's right or wrong, I'll always be by your side.

I may not be there in person, but I am in your heart
Because I know how it feels to fall so far apart.

Don't be upset or hide in fear;
Just realize that I'm still here.

Everyone has shed tears…
I know because I have for years.

You are not weak; no, you are strong!
Never stop climbing; just keep hanging on.

From a Diary

C. S. Burrough

November 1981.

Though the idea of losing my mother was, naturally, unacceptable, it began to occur to me that death may be her ultimate escape from my stepfather and the crippling pain and sadness he caused her. Too much in love to want to cause him any harm, too weak, sick, and impoverished to leave him, she was a prisoner and I, guilty of the selfish fear of losing her, also began on the other hand to secretly wish her dead.

The last time I spoke to her she was surprisingly calm, good humored, high spirited, and remarkably like her old self again, as if she had never even met that man, her husband, her captor, her killer, and I heard her laughing into the phone for the first time in months.

Aunty Vi: I am sorry ("No you aren't."). Well, I'm your godmother, I'll have to take over now ("No you won't.").

David: Will you get any money? ("What money? She didn't have any. Suppose I'll have to pay for the funeral.")

Lady: A wake, darling. That's what she'd expect, straight scotch.

Father: Of course, you can stay here when you come to the funeral - it won't be longer than one night, will it? We'll make a bed up for you in the boys' room.

Straight scotch, wine, gin, beer, Pernod, martini, Creme de Menthe, Baccardi and coke, vodka, brandy... Aspirin. Straight scotch....

∞

My stepmother woke me with a mug of strong, steamy tea. The fat son snored heavily in the other bunk and outside I could hear the drizzle. My father drove me to the funeral parlor where mother lay tarted up in the coffin. Not a word was spoken during the journey and I wondered whether Father would come in to see her. He didn't.

Through the vestibule door was a waiting room with wooden chairs around the walls. From there ran a dark corridor, at the end of which I sensed candlelight. Silence rang in my ears, my breathing became heavier, and everything around me took on a dream-like quality. In the dark corridor, I hesitated. All I could hear was my own heartbeat. As I lifted my right foot to take another brave step further, something touched me on the shoulder and I gasped.

"Can I help you, sir?" asked a small, spindly, balding man from behind thick, ebony framed spectacles.

"Yes," I whispered. "I'm the son of Mrs. Beyers." In my head played a record that mother had brought home for me from the juke-box in a pub she had once worked in, further down the same street as this, her funeral parlor, when I had been about eight or nine: I'm The Son Of Hickory Holler's Tramp. Cath Hall, our next door neighbor, had said to her, "Get that record for him, he likes it." Many times I had played on that street outside the pub, waiting for her to notice me from behind her bar and come out to say hello.

"Oh, I see," he smiled apologetically, adjusting his black tie. "She's through there. Will you be long?"

"Long?" Before I could say any more he scuttled back into the darkness. I continued boldly down the corridor and found Egbert, my stepfather, sobbing over the coffin, his lips slobbering and tears splashing noisily onto something hard. He felt my presence and moved back with a start, glancing nervously at me as if hoping for some kind of forgiveness. I refused him eye contact, but said, "Do you mind leaving us alone for a minute now?"

Reluctantly letting go of the brass handles on the coffin, he edged past me and stood watching from the corridor. He trembled, not with distress or even fear, but with jealousy. Even now he resented me having her to myself for a minute. "I'll meet you in the pub," I heard myself tell him in a controlled, diplomatic tone, and he was gone.

Alone with her, I froze for a few moments until I could breathe more calmly, and then I stepped forward. Dressed in pink with her hair swept up, she wore a contented expression on her face. Almost a faint smile. I sighed, wondering how I ought to be feeling, how she might now feel. Her presence, still plainly evident, comforted me. She had once told me when I was a child, "Don't be afraid of a corpse and be sure to touch it for luck." I bent and kissed her forehead, holding contact for a few, precious moments, then I stood up and gazed at her.

I thought of her. Teaching me how to button up my first cardigan and how to tie my shoelaces. "It'll come with practice; you just need patience." Putting on makeup in the living room mirror. Sitting up late with me during the power cuts because I was afraid of the dark. Throwing my medicine over me when I wouldn't drink it. Phoning me at work when she was drunk. Lending me her nylons for a drag contest. Holding my hand when my pet mouse died. Telling me she had fallen the first time Egbert had blacked her eye.

I licked a salty tear from the side of my mouth and touched her icy hand. Something moved across the room and I saw Lady standing by the door in her rabbit coat. When she came over she looked closely at Mother, took hold of her hand, and said, "Bloody cow still doesn't look a day over 30." We both laughed and made our way over to the bar on the seafront.

Clutching three large gin and tonics we balanced sedately on our bar stools, Lady breaking the atmosphere now and then with a splash of her dry humor, Egbert totally bewildered, me looking out at the cold, grey sea and thinking,

To hell with it, I'm going to Australia! The furthest away place I could think of.

In the funeral car my step-grandmother carried on about the cost of the coffin and Lady squeezed my knee whilst I bit my lip. After two hymns and a reading, the clergyman announced the music my mother had chosen in her last few moments for the funeral. Through crackly speakers we heard Frank Sinatra sing I Did It My Way. Only about 15 people had turned up for the service, most of them locals from the pub. There were no distant relatives. The Yuills' had Catholically and collectively disowned her years before for divorcing. Outside the chapel, pinned onto a wooden stake, were six or seven wreaths. I read the cards on them, and my step-grandmother stood by our funeral car reminding me of the extra cost if we went over the agreed time.

After the service. Eddie, Lady, and I quickly dumped Egbert and his parents and headed for Lucy's bar where Lady made a stream of toasts before departing. We drank on until finally Eddie, the first true love of my life, who had become my mother's other son, the live-in version, wept on my shoulder about how he would never forgive himself for being unable to prevent Egbert from killing her. My mother's death had been recorded as a coronary arrest, explained Eddie, "But it was him that did it to her with his beatings and by feeding her booze when she wasn't meant to be allowed any." Eddie had gone to pieces about it and soon became almost hysterical. I took him home to his room, our old bedroom at mother's house, and returned to him that vast, quilted cloak he had given me to rest my emotions on when I had been 15.

After pouring us both another scotch, he began to fumble troublesomely with his words, eventually becoming quiet, serious, still. I remember lying there with Eddie sitting at my feet, holding my ankle reassuringly.

∞

The Crunch

"I have to tell you," Eddie said, "something she wanted you to know. Please don't interrupt... let me just say it. She asked me to, we talked about it two nights before she went. It's important that you know, so she said."

("What?")

"She wanted you to find out sooner or later that your real father, the real one, was some bloke she ran off with once. A bus driver."

("A what?")

I picked out odd sentences here and there: "She walked out of her marriage for him... They were completely as one... He was killed... Just after conception... He'd sworn never to leave her... She said you were like a picture of him, even used the same phrases as him, that she'd never told anyone else this before, but that she was sure you are him come back, she was certain. But, she said, you went away. You left her."

I heard myself say to Eddie, "But that's wrong... she left me. For Egbert." There was a tense and uncomfortable silence while we drank our scotches; Eddie looked relieved and I felt nonplussed. As if I had already known what he had just told me.

"Oh, come on," Eddie consoled me, "she'd lost her marbles by that stage, there's no need to...." He went on whilst I lay there, shot down by thoughts. If it was true, then my mother would have been my only known blood relative, and I hers because she was adopted. This bus driver's (my) relatives could have been staring me in the face and I wouldn't have known. At one in the morning, I took a taxi back to father's house and tried to mentally strike that day off my calendar forever. Cancel it.

There had been virtually nothing of my mother's left in the house for me to keep. Egbert had either sold or thrown away everything that may have meant anything to me. So I took her original engagement ring, given to her by my father. The emerald had been pried out, but I would have the empty clasp removed and the gold band adjusted to fit me. I have worn it ever since and never again contacted my stepfather.

The following morning, boarding the train back to London, I told my father and stepmother I would be leaving England for an indefinite period. My stepmother kissed me on the cheek and my father shook my hand formally as do company chairmen when a long-standing employee retires.

A week later I phoned Aunty Vi and we said our farewells, then I sat with David for a few minutes. He was minding my belongings, as I had no idea how long I would be away, assuming that I would actually return. We hugged tightly for a moment and then I was gone.

I often wonder what my homeland is like. And who my blood relatives are.

I'm a Really Big Flyswatter

Jill Eisnaugle

"Something just doesn't feel right," I told myself on the evening of February 11, 2012. That night marked one month since the emotional abuse I endured over the course of five years had reached its apex. It is hard to describe, even now, the emotions I felt as I sat on the loveseat, consumed by feelings of emptiness, shame, guilt, and confusion over how someone I once called a co-worker and friend could degrade my self-worth so much.

"Why do I feel such confusion?" I asked myself. I knew I had done the right thing by refusing to remain silent and telling the abuser's boss about the torment I endured, but by that same token, I also knew that five years of harassment from a man twice my age took its toll on my emotions and heart. It was a Saturday and around 6:30 pm when I decided I needed to do something, so I opened my laptop and searched for online counseling. Scrolling the list of available experts, I happened upon the biography of Mary Lee Palmer, a Licensed Clinical Social Worker with years of experience dealing with just the scenarios I had survived. Something deep within my heart told me that she was the one to help me regain control of my life.

Admittedly, I never considered the option of therapy sessions by chat, phone, or email prior to that night. In fact, I never thought I needed therapy at all. Throughout my life, I was the one that others turned to for advice or support in times of crisis. I always tried my best to help others and myself when situations arose that were less than ideal. The emotional trauma was something unlike anything I ever knew, however, and the only thought that crossed my mind was that I needed help. At that hour, on a weekend, I knew not much was available. Though, at the time, I saw that my inner voice was steering me in the wrong direction too often, so I decided to take a chance.

The chat session began with introductions and a description of the trauma I faced. Mary Lee immediately assured me that what happened was not my fault and that I did the right thing by addressing my concerns with the man's boss. This alone put my mind at ease. Then, as the chat continued, she said, "Think of this man as a gnat… an annoying little gnat that you can flick away and watch as he gets smaller and smaller on your horizon."

After the chat therapy session ended, I felt a lot better. Mary Lee and I chatted again a few days later, and every time she mentioned the gnat reference, I could not help but smile. It was a way of looking at things that I'd never before heard and yet, something I could picture in my mind.

As time went on and our chats continued, I took the concept of flicking away the gnat and began seeing myself as a really big flyswatter. The phrase, "He's an annoying little gnat and I'm a really big flyswatter," became commonplace in every chat, phone, or email therapy session we shared. At the time, however, what I did not realize was that I created the flyswatter part of that phrase and, by doing so, I showed and admitted to myself that I am bigger than any problem life may throw at me.

Years have now passed since the confusion, guilt, shame, and emptiness first took hold of my life. I am happy, healthy, and whole again. Thanks to Mary Lee's guidance, my abuser is no longer visible on my mental horizon; I have regained full control of my destiny and I will likely smile for the rest of eternity every time I think of a gnat or use a flyswatter.

Sometimes, the best and most meaningful advice is devoid of big psychological terms or textbook definitions, but instead filled with simple and relatable concepts that frame a difficult situation in a different light. On some level, I will always see myself as a really big flyswatter, and thanks to Mary Lee Palmer's "gnat-tastic" advice, I will be eternally grateful!

From PTSD to Happiness

Henriette Eiby Christensen

I met my ex-husband when I was 32. I was a single mother and had just moved back to Denmark after seven years in the US with my three-year-old son. I was working from home as the sole employee of a new dating business sending parties of six strangers out to dinner.

He seemed absolutely perfect. Tall, handsome, and considerate. He offered to come do my dishes because I had this terrible cold that wouldn't go away, and I'd told him on the phone that my dishes were stacked to the ceiling. He arrived with flowers, fruit, and vitamins, and he blew me away. He seemed to be exactly what I was looking for. Smart, spiritual, creative, and prepared to take care of me and my son. I just wanted to be a stay-at-home mom.

The funny thing (in retrospect) is that I'd just read Robin Norwood's book *Women Who Love too Much* and loved it – it had made me fall in love with life, and I'd just joined a support group which I promptly decided to quit because, "the others were much worse off than I, and I'd just found the perfect man." 17 years of mental agony ensued; 12 with him and five more trying to figure out what had happened and why I felt so bad and kept feeling like the world would be a better place without me in it.

I had been truly relieved when he'd left, so why did I feel like that? Sure, any divorce is a loss of heavy duty illusions of, "for better or for worse," "happily ever after," and having the, "perfect house and family." You will have to go through a period of grief and regrets no matter how much you want to leave and how much you feel it is the right thing to do. A divorce can very well leave you with a feeling of failure, of not being good enough, smart or giving enough, flexible enough, understanding enough, and so on.

I understood that, but the depression lingered on and on. Nothing would lighten it up. In retrospect, it is very clear that I was completely overworked, overwhelmed by the responsibilities of single parenthood and finishing school at the same time. Preparing three meals a day for three kids 365 days a year, having to find a new job, sleepless nights, and headaches. Not caring about taking showers, my appearance, my hair, or what I ate. Pills....

Only just able to put food on the table for my kids and making sure they got up in the mornings.

Considering if I wanted to live or not....

I felt completely and utterly alone.

At one point before my ex and I split, I'd asked my doctor how long my body could handle being so stressed before I'd get sick. All he said was, "Don't do that," which wasn't enough for me to take the necessary steps toward leaving. Asking a question like that is an obvious pointer that something is very wrong, but I still wasn't willing to see it or listen to it. I was already stressed almost to the max before the split up.

∞

Overcoming Stress and PTSD

Only very slowly did the nightmares subside. I remember one of them vividly.

I was on a beach. I had killed my ex-husband and chopped him to pieces, put him in a garbage bag, and dumped him in a container.

This was not the scary part.

I woke up terrified not that I'd killed him and chopped him up, but that I would be found out and I would not be able to be with my children.

At a time when I was the worst off, I could see huge woodlice the size of big dogs crawling across the ceiling when I woke up at night. I knew they weren't real, but I could see them even when I looked right at them. I have not seen this symptom in any descriptions of PTSD. I've only seen it mentioned in connection with delirium tremens (also known as the shakes) and drug rehabilitation. I wasn't drinking and I wasn't doing drugs except for an occasional sleeping pill.

It goes to show how stressed I really was.

It was the scariest thing I have experienced. I never mentioned it to anybody, not even my doctor, because I was afraid it would be used against me.

I didn't admit to it until our problems were all gone many years later.

How does one move on from there?

I had the strongest need to understand what had happened, so I started reading and writing. I read every book on positive thinking and the law of attraction I could find. I did every exercise I could dig up. I found meditations on YouTube. You name it, I did it. If you have ever had to quit an addiction you know how much it takes. The stamina and the will power. I wanted to understand with every fiber of my body so I would never get stuck like that again. I wrote books on telltale signs of bad relationships and then books on everything I learned about moving on. Now I am finally writing about the good relationship. Check out my 110 Ways Series.

Henriette Eiby Christensen
www.110ways.com
http://tinyurl.com/110ways-amazon
https://www.facebook.com/110Ways

Final Thoughts
Jennifer-Crystal Johnson

As with the first issue of Soul Vomit, reading about all of these different imagined and real scenarios, I spent many hours crying as I edit, remembering the pain, and recalling my own past experiences with domestic violence.

Everyone's journey is different, during and after an experience like this. Though many of the emotions themselves are similar, we each have our own path of healing and rediscovering ourselves to travel.

May you travel well and have a safe and wildly successful trip!

If you enjoyed the book, were touched by its message, or simply wish to show support, please leave us a review on Amazon! It's greatly appreciated. *70% of proceeds go to DV charities.*

Past issues of Soul Vomit:
Soul Vomit: Beating Domestic Violence, 2012

More information:
www.SoulVomit.com
www.BrokenPublications.com
www.JenniferCrystalJohnson.com

Contributor Information

A. J. Huffman
Just Words, p. 116

A. J. Huffman is a poet and freelance writer in Daytona Beach, Florida. She has previously published six collections of poetry, all available on Amazon.com. She has also published her work in numerous national and international literary journals. She is currently the editor for six online poetry journals for Kind of a Hurricane Press (www.KindOfAHurricanePress.com). Find more about A. J. Huffman, including additional information and links to her work at:

www.facebook.com/amy.huffman.5
Twitter: @poetess222

Andrea Barton
Arrhythmia, p. 114; *Butchered*, p. 128; *Stepping Backward*, p. 110; *Watermark*, p. 46

Andrea Barton is a mother, a daughter, a poet, a high school English teacher, and an editor, in that order. She has had work published in *Labletter*, *The Cleave* webzine, the book *The Berlin Turnpike* (about human trafficking), and the *Lewis and Clark Literary Review*. In 2010, she published *Leaves Pasted Akimbo*, a book of poems for and about her daughter, and is currently finishing a new book, *The Was of You, Poems and Essays in Grief Because We've All Been There*. Andrea lives in a semi-bucolic suburb of Hartford, CT with her 11-year-old daughter ("Girlycue") and their cat Lola, who occasionally comes in to eat.

April Salzano

Kneeling There, p. 111; *Second Thoughts*, p. 156; *Sleepwalker*, p. 67

April Salzano teaches college writing in Pennsylvania and is working on her first several collections of poetry and an autobiographical novel on raising a child with Autism. Her work has appeared in *Poetry Salzburg, Convergence, Ascent Aspirations, The Rainbow Rose, The Camel Saloon, The Applicant, The Mindful Word, The Weekender Magazine, Deadsnakes, Winemop, Daily Love, WIZ, Visceral Uterus, Crisis Chronicles, Windmills*, and is forthcoming in *Inclement, Poetry Quarterly, Decompression, Work to a Calm*, and *Bluestem*. The author also serves as co-editor for several online journals at Kind of a Hurricane Press.

C. S. Burrough

From A Diary, p. 161

Sydneysider C. S. Burrough began life in the UK. After studying Performing Arts full-time, he worked on West End theatre productions and toured shows internationally for 16 years, settling in Australia in the early 1980s. He has written and published since 1989 in anthologies and newspapers, having produced two full-length works and numerous novellas and short stories, and is also a prolific reviewer of books. His latest novel, the historical saga *Or Forever Be Damned*, was released August 5th, 2014 by Silky Oak Press as an eBook. Its paperback release was September 2014.

Facebook: https://www.facebook.com/csburrough
Twitter: @csburrough
Amazon: https://www.amazon.com/author/csburrough

Dalian Graylocke

Not Innocent (The Second Time), p. 75; *Shade of Blue*, p. 65

Dalian Graylocke is a great lover of music, which none of her stories would exist without. She is passionate about the emotional subtext of her characters and stories that ring true. Her first novel, *Metaphor*, is due to be released at the end of 2014. The beginning of the novel is a song she wrote and the chapter titles are all lines from the lyrics. She lives with her husband in Colorado, and you can check out her songs at www.soundcloud.com/tomikaiser.

Debbie Lechtman

Monsters, p. 43

Debbie Lechtman is a 23-year-old writer (primarily fiction) and artist based in Austin, Texas. Her work has been featured in a number of literary magazines and anthologies. You can find out more at:
www.DebbieLechtman.com.

Eric Michelson

Furnishing Gratitude, p. 140

In the end, all we've ever had was an end to call our own.

Helen Carl

Haunted, p. 141

When I was 13, my family moved from our home in Baltimore to Pueblo, Colorado. Severe depression reared its ugly head, brought out by the stress of the move. But my family was there to help me through it. My freshman year in high school I met my husband, Patrick. I married him after I graduated. Then the depression returned with a vengeance and I was diagnosed with severe bi-polar disorder, borderline schizophrenia. And as always, my family was there to help me through it. My parents are both writers; my dad writes horror and sci-fi. So I took a page from his book and started writing short stories to help me better deal with the parts of my mind that I couldn't understand.

Henriette Eiby Christensen
From PTSD to Happiness, p. 169

Henriette Eiby Christensen is a mother of three, teacher, and author. Having experienced toxic relationships and how difficult it is to break free, she now has a burning desire to change the world for the better by providing the necessary communication skills and awareness that are sorely lacking in many relationships.

Through her extensive research and experience on the lecture circuit, her help blogs, counseling, *110 Ways* series, Facebook pages & groups, and raising her own children in romantically toxic environments, she believes that the road to recovery starts at home with education and compassion. Compassion not only for others, but most certainly for yourself.

She lives in Denmark with her children and her new love. You can find out more about her books at www.110Ways.com.

Jaclyn Crombie
Little Creatures, p. 47

I am a prose and poetry writer currently residing in Bunbury, Western Australia, and am completing a Bachelor of Arts Honors on the subject of Young Adult

Literature. My story, *Little Creatures*, under the alternative title, *Waiting to Run*, was shortlisted and received the award of Highly Commended in the 2012 Edith Cowan University South West Writing Competition.

Jennifer-Crystal Johnson

Beautiful Numb, p. 118; *Foreword*, p. 7; *Set Me Free*, p. 54; *Simply Me*, p. 134

Jennifer-Crystal Johnson is originally from Germany, but was raised all over. She has published one novella under her former last name, *The Outside Girl: Perception is Reality* (PublishAmerica, 2005 - out of print), a poetry book, *Napkin Poetry* (Broken Publications, 2010), and a collection of poetry, art, and prose called *Strangers with Familiar Faces* (Broken Publications, 2011). More recent releases include *If You're Human Don't Open the Door* (Broken Publications, 2012, Kindle only) and *The Ten Pillars of a Happy Relationship* (Broken Publications, 2012).

Her poetry and short stories have been featured on Every Writer's Resource and various other publications in print and online. She currently works as the Managing Editor for *phati'tude* Literary Magazine, does assistant editing and publishing work at Amberjack Publishing, and works with freelance clients all over the world to help them self-publish through Amazon in print and eBook formats.

She lives in the Pacific Northwest with her three kids and four cats. To find out more, please visit:
www.JenniferCrystalJohnson.com
www.facebook.com/JenniferCrystalJohnson
Twitter: @brokenpoet

Jessica Drummond

Coming Down, p. 68; *Perfect Grave*, p. 59

Jessica Drummond is a 23-year-old music and word addict, previously unpublished.

Jill Eisnaugle

A Different Tune, p. 69; *Her Courage*, p. 138; *I'm a Really Big Flyswatter*, p. 167; *Ode to Slime*, p. 130; *Wounded Butterfly*, p. 119

Jill Eisnaugle is the author of five books. Her work has been featured by Hallmark, *Chicken Soup for the Soul*, and various magazines. To learn more, please visit: http://www.authorsden.com/jillaeisnaugle

Katie Rendon Kahn

Between the Lines, p. 53; *Man of the House*, p. 113; *Phantom Limb*, p. 74; *Young Brides*, p. 38

Katie Rendon Kahn returns after having two poems in the first anthology, *Soul Vomit: Beating Domestic Violence*. She lives on the Florida Panhandle with her husband and three kids. She has also had work published in *The Blackwater Review*, *Diverse Voices Quarterly*, and *The Barefoot Review*.

Lee Ann Perez

Third Floor, p. 39

(No bio submitted.)

Lee Smiley

A Coup in Chuckistan, p. 29

Lee Smiley lives in northwest Tennessee. His work has appeared in *Ghostlight*, *The Fear of Monkeys*, and *Gone with the Dirt: Undead Dixie*. Visit him at his website www.LeeSmiley.com and follow him on Twitter @lee_smiley. In addition, if you or anyone you know shares a similar experience of abuse, please contact the National Coalition Against Domestic Violence at www.ncadv.org.

Marilyn Oakley
Bruises On My Heart, p. 123; *Survivor of My Enemy*, p. 28

A Wisconsin native, Marilyn Oakley is an author and songwriter. She has written songs on domestic abuse as well. You can hear them here:

https://soundcloud.com/marilyn-oakley/say-hello-to-goodbye
https://soundcloud.com/marilyn-oakley/house-without-a-home

Domestic violence and abuse is a subject that needs to be dealt with, talked about, and shared.

Maxine Moncrieffe
Alone Again, p. 58; *As I Rise to Face the New Day*, p. 125; *Cleaning Up*, p. 158; *Freedom*, p. 132; *One Step Over, Please*, p. 117

I am 42 years of age, born in Brooklyn, NY to parents from Jamaica. My mother was a published poet and encouraged me to continue writing upon reading my first Haiku, written at the age of five.

I have raised three children to the best of my ability, with certain flaws due to the domestic violence that encompassed my life. I watched my mother being beaten by my father on a regular basis. I also watched my mother fight back with every ounce of her being. I grew up and came from a very hostile and violent background. Needless to say, it was also the story of my life, as the abuse was so severe and consistent that it took most of my life to break free of it.

Through my poetry I find and express myself until release and peace take over. Maybe through my experiences and poetry, I may touch one person. Letting them know there is hope, freedom, and life worth pursuing and living for. Life during and after abuse is not easy, but well worth all the sacrifices and efforts.

Not only do I hope that my works are enjoyed, but I hope that they give a window into what domestic violence can do and that recovery, hope, freedom, and life are indeed possible during and after the storm.

Nicholas P. Anthony
Penumbra, p. 55

I am a fourth year student at Santa Clara University, where I am studying English and Communications. I have known women who are subjected to physical abuse or who have experienced it in their life, and their stories have impacted my own life. It is a subject that has become very dear to me. One that I write about because that is the only way I know how to raise awareness.

Tiffany Lewis
The Long Walk Home, p. 135

Tiffany has been writing since her adolescence. Her passion for writing took a backseat to a career in education as well as her personal education. Although her love for children is unwavering, she is determined to start her career as a writer.

Tiffany was honored to have her work published for the first time in May, 2011. Since then, her work has been featured in many books and online publications. Ranging from fiction to non-fiction, murder to relationships, Tiffany's range as a writer is wide and deep.

Tiffany writes for readers and often wants their full input as she creates her work. "It is my job to satisfy readers, so everything they say about my work is invaluable and I use it to make myself and my writing better."

Tiffany has taken a vow to never publish her own work because she feels that there is nothing better than having another person love it and want to say that they published it first.

She continues to write avidly and seek publication opportunities.

Joshua "Weck" Woeckener
Cream Soda, p. 25

Joshua "Weck" Woeckener began writing poetry on internet writer's forums. As he became more comfortable with his work, he ventured into the world of Slam Poetry, adopting the moniker "Weck." Through this, he fell in love with both the written and spoken word. He is a former member of the SpeakTuMePoetry Experience, a spoken word performance troupe based in Fort Walton Beach, FL. He is also an active participant in Say the Word, an open mic at The French Quarter Grill where he currently resides in Valparaiso, FL.

William McKnight
Darkness, p. 15

William McKnight, J.D., knows about domestic violence. He has worked in the Criminal Justice system for over 30 years as Criminal Defense Lawyer, Police Officer, Investigator, and college instructor of Criminal Justice courses. He also spent five years in Iraq with the US State Department's Civilian Police Project. He is a regular contributing freelance writer with TextBrokers and has written articles in several periodicals, including PoliceOne magazine, expert articles for the Oregon Criminal Defense Lawyers' Association, and a non-fiction book, *Blue Bonnets O'er the Border*. McKnight's life experience brings a flavor of realism to his writing.

Acknowledgments

A big thank you goes out to each and every contributor who took the time to send in their work and give their words of encouragement for this project. Without the writers and artists who share their stories, the anthology would not exist – I appreciate everyone putting in so much of themselves, even at their own risk, to help raise awareness and reach out to domestic violence victims and survivors.

This is the second *Soul Vomit* anthology published by Broken Publications. Though it's still somewhat new, it is my sincerest hope to publish many more like it, all focusing on different topics and aspects of the journeys victims and survivors are on.

The goals for the anthology and future hopes and dreams have been made pretty clear already, but none of it will be possible without future contributions from writers and artists, so I hope that these works are received well and that future anthologies will also be received with such immense support!

To learn more and stay connected, please visit:

www.SoulVomit.com
www.BrokenPublications.com
www.JenniferCrystalJohnson.com

To follow on Twitter:
@BrokenPublctns
@BrokenPoet

To connect on Facebook:
Facebook.com/SoulVomitAnthology
Facebook.com/BrokenPublications
Facebook.com/BrokenPoetJen

www.ingramcontent.com/pod-product-compliance
Lightning Source LLC
Chambersburg PA
CBHW060110260626
47160CB00005B/1848